# KINDLE VOYAGE

## USERS MANUAL

### A Guide to Getting Started, Advanced Tips and Tricks, and Finding Unlimited Free Books

By Steve Weber



Published by Stephen W. Weber
ISBN 978-1-936560-25-7

# Free Kindle books, all you can eat!

**Kindle Buffet** is a daily website that features a hand-picked list of great Kindle books being offered free or deeply discounted. Visit www.KindleBuffet.com

**Above: The home page of Kindle Buffet, which features daily Kindle freebies and discounts.**

# Contents

# Introduction

Amazon's newest Kindle, the Voyage, sets the gold standard for eReaders. It's noticeably lighter and smaller than its predecessor, the Paperwhite. When you consider the quality of the hardware plus the richness of Amazon's unsurpassed library of content, it's an unbeatable combination. Nothing else even comes close, and nothing can threaten the Voyage's dominance for the foreseeable future.

The biggest improvement the Voyage brings is its incredible display, which equals the sharpness and contrast of the printed page. When you compare the Voyage and Paperwhite side by side, the Paperwhite's display is fuzzy and blotchy.

Yes, the Voyage costs a bit extra, but it's worth every penny to the discriminating reader.

The Voyage is the perfect e-reader, whether you're sitting on the beach or reclined in bed. With no glare in bright sunlight, and the built-in backlight, you can read for hours on end with no eyestrain whatsoever, and no worrying about battery stamina. Lighter in weight than most small paperbacks, the Voyage allows you to concentrate on reading, without distractions like email.

But reading text is only the beginning. The built-in dictionary provides quick access to definitions, and its link to Wikipedia and the X-Ray feature provide instant explanations of characters, settings, and more. You can read the complete text of footnotes without losing your place. There are no confusing buttons. Everything is handled by the intuitive touchscreen interface.

And, of course, the Voyage can hold a huge library of your favorite books—more than a thousand—and instant access to new books. The Whispersync feature syncronizes your last-read location, bookmarks, and annotations across all your devices—other Kindles and Kindle apps available for smartphones and computers.

You have access to more than a million titles priced at $4.99 and less, not to mention a treasure trove of newspapers and magazines. And at participating public libraries, you can borrow Kindle books at no charge, and you don't even have to visit the library. You can lend your Kindle books to other Kindle users for up to two weeks.

If you should lose your Kindle, no worries—your entire library is backed up at no charge in Amazon's "Cloud" wireless storage system. Never worry about misplacing or losing a book again.

You can also use your Kindle to view personal documents. You can email Word, PDF and other documents directly to your Kindle and read them in Kindle format.

**Above: The Voyage, in the foreground, is slightly smaller and lighter than the Paperwhite, and has noticeably improved sharpness, contrast, and brightness. For the first time, an eReader equals the printed page. The Voyage's display surface is flush with the bezel frame, instead of the Paperwhite's angled edge, which could collect dust and dirt.**

The Voyage is invaluable for the whole family. You can encourage kids' love of reading with thousands of free classics like *Alice in Wonderland*, *Black Beauty*, *Peter Pan*, and *Treasure Island*. With Kindle FreeTime, you can encourage your kids to read even more, with all-you-can-eat access to great books, while you receive progress reports on the total time spent reading and number of words looked up.

# CHAPTER I

THE year 1866 was signalised by a remarkable incident, a mysterious and puzzling phenomenon, which doubtless no one has yet forgotten. Not to mention rumours which agitated the maritime population and excited the public mind, even in the interior of continents, seafaring men were particularly excited. Merchants, common sailors, captains of vessels, skippers, both of Europe and America, naval officers of all countries, and the Governments of several States on the two continents, were deeply interested in the matter.

For some time past vessels had been met by "an enormous thing," a long object, spindle-shaped, occasionally phosphorescent, and infinitely larger

1 min left in chapter                              1%

kindle

**Above: Thinner than a pencil, the Voyage introduces a new page-advance system called PagePress, which works when the reader squeezes the side of the bezel. The reader can also tap or flick the side of the screen to page forward or back.**

With the built-in Vocabulary Builder, kids can quiz themselves with flashcards to strengthen their word retention.

The Voyage supports illustrated children's books, too, with pop-up text and Panel View, allowing them to read comic books panel by panel.

You can organize your library into customized collections, or categories, to easily access any book you're searching for.

You can customize the Voyage for use in English, Spanish, Brazilian Portuguese, French, German, Italian, Japanese, and Simplified Chinese. Simply select the language you're most comfortable with, and enjoy instant dictionary lookups in any of these languages.

Of course, you'll receive personalized recommendations from Amazon for great new books, right on your device. Offers are displayed on the screensaver and the bottom of the home screen while you're not using your device.

# 1 ▶ FAST START GUIDE

Your Kindle Voyage will be partially charged when you take it out of the box. You can charge the battery with the supplied USB cable, connected to a computer. Fully charging the battery normally takes four to six hours.

To charge your device without a computer, you'll need to purchase a compatible wall adapter for the USB cable. Connecting to a wall adapter will reduce your charging time to four hours or less.

## *Charging Your Voyage*

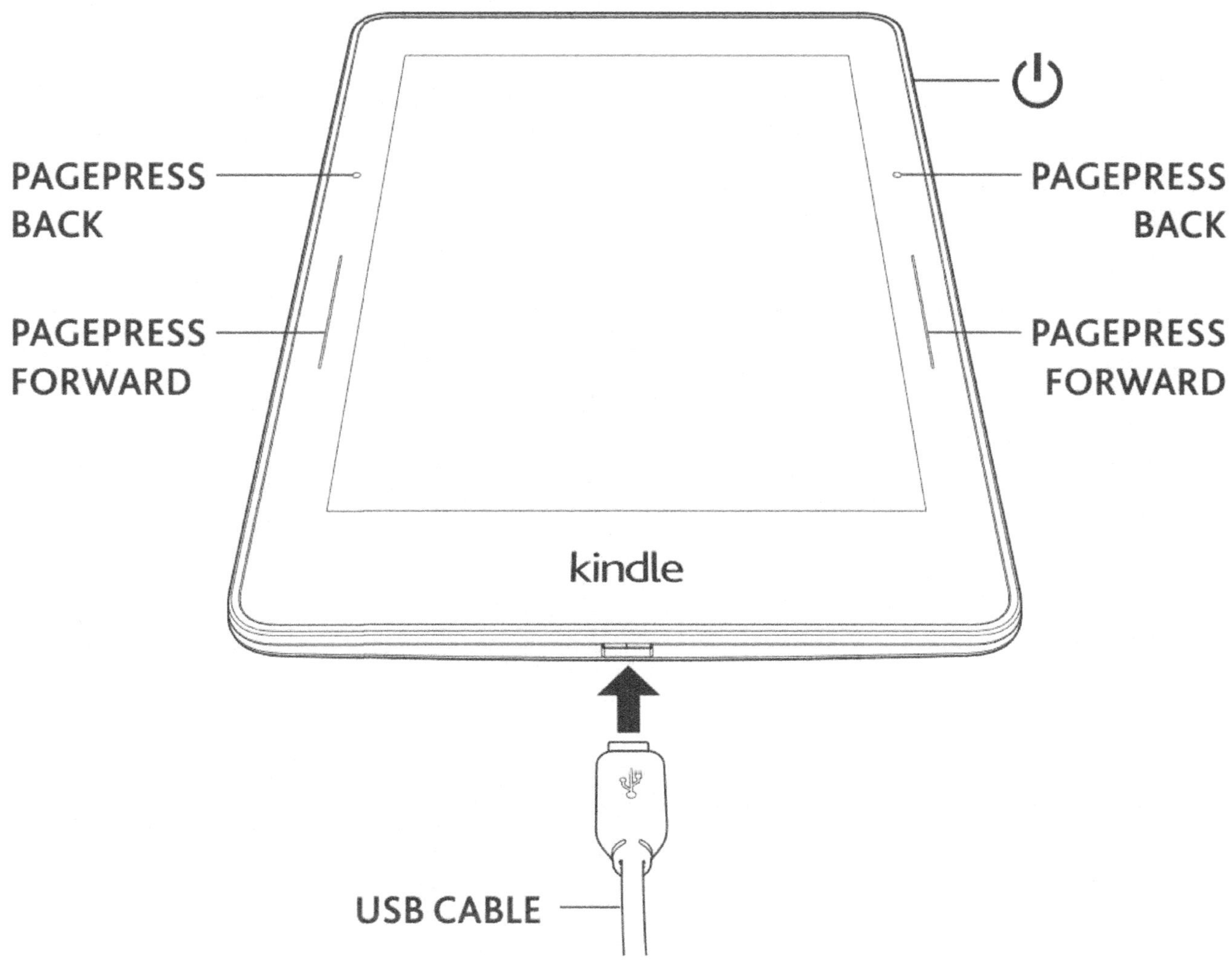

**TIP:** To conserve battery life, place your Kindle into sleep mode after you're finished using it. Press and release the power button to put your device in sleep mode.

When your device is charging, a **lightning bolt** 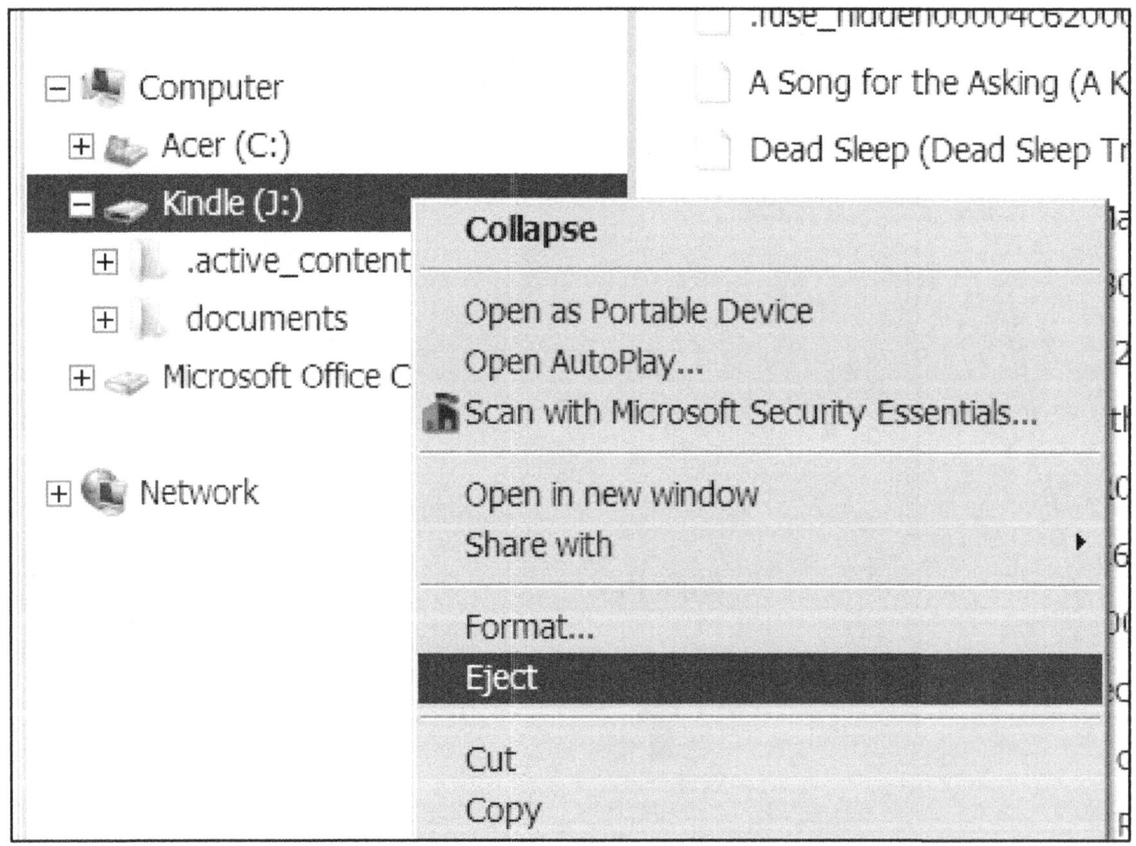 appears on the battery icon at the top of the **Home** screen. While your Kindle is charging, the charge indicator light glows amber. When your device is fully charged, the indicator light glows green.

When you connect your device to a computer, the screen will indicate the device is in "USB Drive Mode."

You can use your Voyage while it's connected to the computer if you "eject" the device from your computer so that it exits USB Drive Mode.

- **For Windows computers:** Click on My Computer, then right-click on your Kindle.

- **For Macs:** Click the Eject button beside the Kindle in any Finder window, or drag the Kindle from the Desktop to the Trash.

**Above: At left: On your computer, right-click on the Kindle to safely eject the device from USB Drive Mode. Now you can use the device while connected—or safely disconnect the device from your computer.**

## *If your battery won't stay charged*

If your Voyage takes longer than six hours to fully charge—or won't stay charged—follow these steps:

- **Ensure you have a connection at both ends of your USB cord.** Sometimes the wire fraus or the metal tip is damaged, resulting in a bad connection. Try using a different USB cord.

- **Place your Voyage in Sleep Mode after you're finished reading.** Press the **Power** button on the back of your Kindle to conserve battery life.

- **Turn off Wireless**. (This turns on **Airplane Mode**, shown by the indicator ✈ . This conserves battery power, but you won't be able to browse the Web or purchase, download or sync Kindle content.

  1. From the Home screen, tap the **Menu** ☰ icon, then tap Settings.

  2. Next to **Airplane Mode**, tap **Off**. The switch moves to the **On** position, indicating that **Airplane Mode** is on, and your **WiFi** or **3G** connection is off.

- **Charge your device by connecting to a wall adapter.** Sometimes a USB connection with a computer doesn't fully charge the Kindle.

- **Restart your device.** Unplug the USB cable, then press and hold the power button for seven seconds. On your screen, a Power dialog box appears. Tap Restart. When your Kindle restarts, connect the USB cable to your Voyage and your computer, and verify your device is charging.

## Registering Your Voyage

To download content to your Voyage, you'll need to establish a wireless connection and register the device to your Amazon account. Registering enables you to download your content from other Kindle devices and reading apps.

1. From the **Home** screen tap the **Menu** ☰ icon, then tap **Settings**.

2. Tap Registration.

3. Choose the Amazon account you want to use with your Voyage.

   - **If you already have an Amazon account:** Tap this option. Enter your Amazon email address and password. Tap **Register**. When finished, your name will appear as the Registered User.

   - **If you don't have an Amazon account:** Tap this option and follow the instruction on the screen to set up a new Amazon account.

## *Setting Up Wi-Fi*

A wireless network provides fast downloads of your Kindle books and other content. To view the available Wi-Fi networks:

1.  From the **Home** screen, tap the **Menu** ☰ icon, then tap **Settings**.

2.  Select the name of the Wi-Fi network you want to use. If a lock icon appears next to the network name, it requires a password.

Once you've connected to a network, the Wi-Fi status indicator at the top of the screen indicates the signal strength.

**Above: The Voyage shows all Wi-Fi networks within range of your device.**

Your Voyage will automatically find and connect with networks you've joined previously. The wireless indicator is located near the top-right corner of your screen, next to the battery indicator. A display of three bars indicates that your device is connected to a network with a strong signal. A series of dashes indicates your device isn't connected.

## Connect to WiFi manually

If the WiFi network you want to use isn't listed on your device, you can type in the name of the network.

1.  From **Home**, tap the **Menu** icon, ▬ and then **Settings**.

2.  Tap **WiFi Networks** to display the list of detected networks.

3.  Tap **Other**.

4.  Using the onscreen keyboard, type the **Network Name**. (If you don't know the name of your network, contact your Internet Service Provider.)

5.  Tap the **Password** box and enter your password.

6.  Tap **Connect**.

## Trouble Connecting to a Wi-Fi Network

If you're unable to connect to a home network you've used previously, follow this procedure:

1.  Turn off your Wi-Fi router and modem. Wait 30 seconds.

2.  Press and hold your Voyage's **Power** button, then tap **Restart**.

3.  Turn on your modem and wait while it restarts.

4.  Turn on your router; wait for it to restart.

5.  After your devices restart, try connecting to your Wi-Fi network again.

## Turning on Airplane Mode

You can turn off your 3G or Wi-Fi connection to conserve battery power or to use your Voyage while traveling on aircraft.

1.  From **Home**, tap the **Menu** ▬ icon, then tap **Settings**.

2.  Next to **Airplane** mode, tap **Off**. The switch will move to the **On** position. Now Airplane mode is on, and your wireless connection is off.

## Connecting to a Mobile Network

If you purchased the 3G Voyage, it provides free 3G wireless service with no monthly fees or annual contracts.

Your Voyage automatically switches to Wi-Fi when available, which provides greater download speeds. If you're out of range of Wi-Fi, your device switches to a mobile connection when enabled.

## Basic Navigation

You'll need just a few basic controls to use your Voyage. Turn on the device by pressing the power button on the back of the device.

To turn off your device, press and hold the power button for seven seconds.

After a few minutes of inactivity, your device will enter sleep mode to conserve power. A screen saver will be displayed, which requires no power. Press the power button to awaken your Voyage, and swipe your finger across the bottom of the screen to begin using the device.

### *Navigating with the PagePress feature.*

Gently squeeze the side of the bezel to activate the PagePress feature. The sensor on the top (shaped like a dot) returns you to the previous page, and the bottom sensor (shaped like a line) turns a page ahead. A subtle vibration lets you know when you've triggered a page turn. You can use the same controls to navigate the home screen.

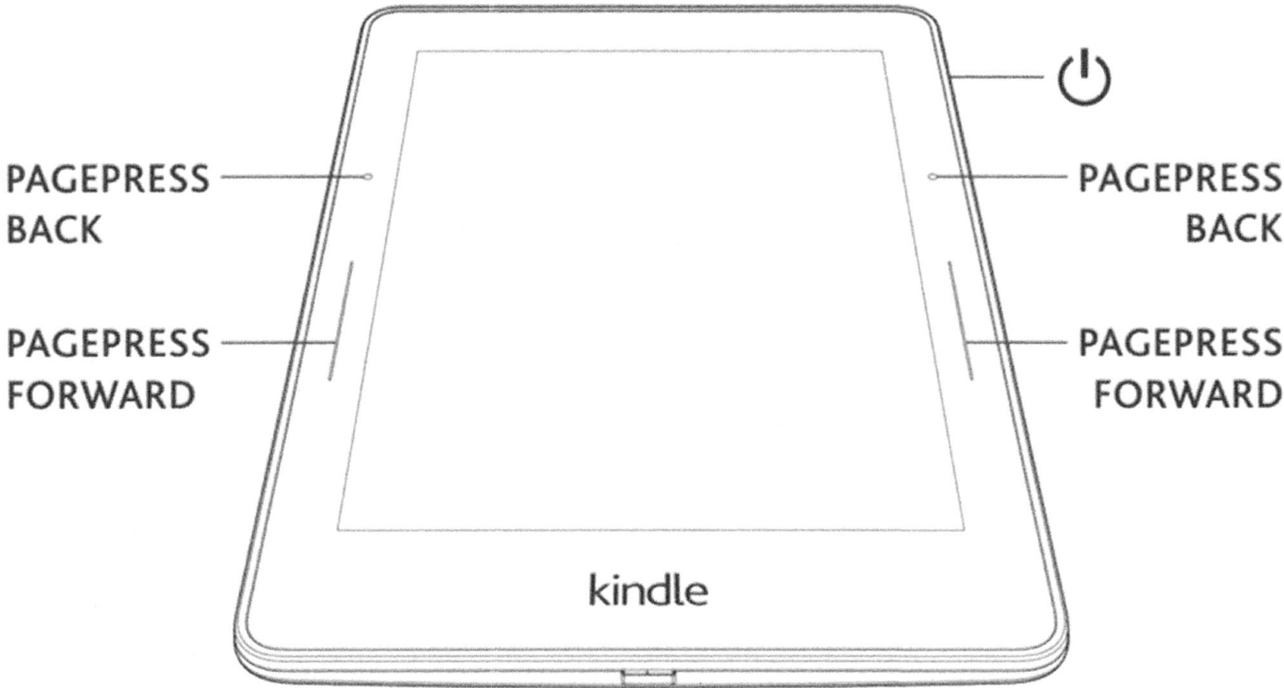


You can also move a page forward or a pack back by tapping on the right or left side of the screen.

## *Navigating the Home Screen*

The **Home** screen, pictured below, shows a list of the content stored on your Voyage. Here you can manage and organize your Kindle books and other content.

To go to the **Home** screen, tap the **Home** 🏠 icon. (If the **Home** icon isn't visible, tap the top of your screen, and the **Home** icon appears in the toolbar.)

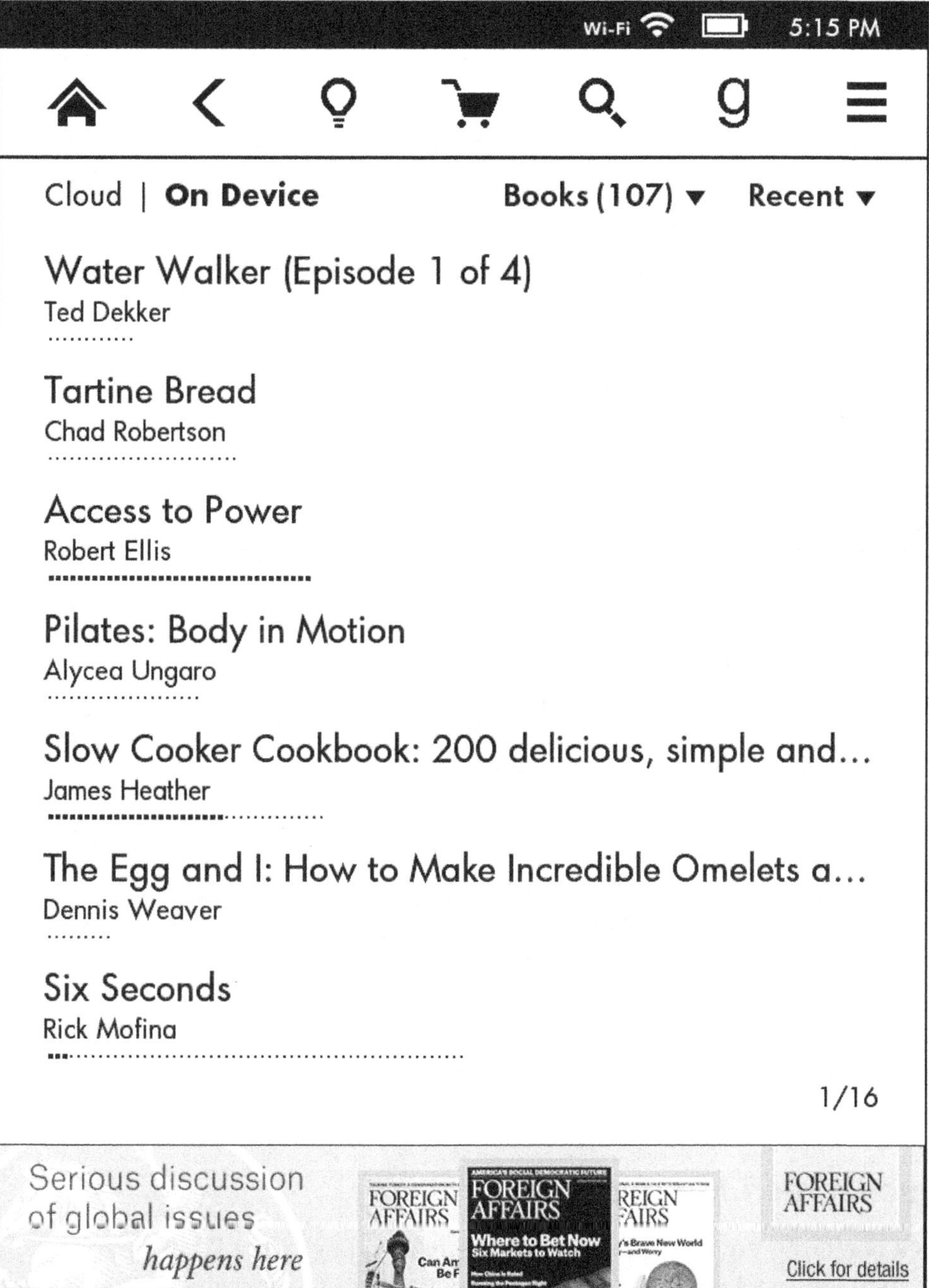


**Above: The Voyage Home screen in "List View," which shows the titles stored on the device. An alternate view, "Cover View," shows the cover images of the books.**

Near the top left corner of the **Home** screen, there's a tab for **On Device** and another tab for **Cloud**.

- **Open a book:** Tap the **On Device** tab to view the items downloaded to your device. Tap a title to open it.

- **Remove a book:** Press and hold the title, then tap **Remove from Device**. The title is erased from your Voyage and added to the **Cloud** tab, where it's available for downloading again.

- **Sort books and other items:** You can view your list of titles sorted by **Recent**, **Title**, **Author** or **Collections**.

- **Filter by type of document:** Tap **My Items**, then tap **All Items**, **Books**, **Periodicals**, **Docs**, or **Active Content**.

- **Search for a book or periodical:** Tap the **Magnifying Glass** icon in the toolbar. Tap **My Items** to search your library. Or widen your search to include the **Kindle Store**, **Dictionary**, or **Wikipedia**.

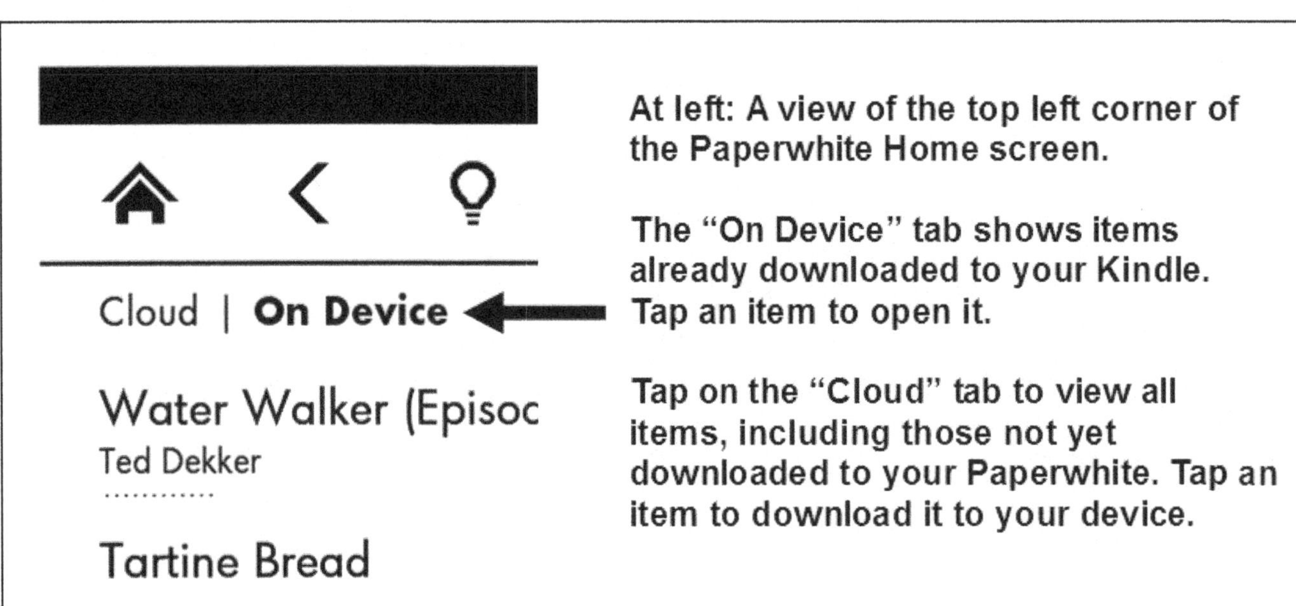


At left: A view of the top left corner of the Paperwhite Home screen.

The "On Device" tab shows items already downloaded to your Kindle. Tap an item to open it.

Tap on the "Cloud" tab to view all items, including those not yet downloaded to your Paperwhite. Tap an item to download it to your device.

## *Navigating With the Touchscreen Interface*

Just as you'd do with a paperback book, the Voyage allows you to easily turn pages in a Kindle book. Tapping almost anywhere on the display area will bring you to the following page. Tap the left side of the screen to return to the previous page.

The touchscreen navigation works whether you're holding your Voyage in **Portrait Mode** (like a small paperback) or in **Landscape Mode** (like a coffee-table book).

**Portrait Mode** ⟶

**Landscape Mode**

Tap this area to display the toolbar

Tap this area to go to the next page

◂ Tap this area to go
to the previous page

Tap this area to display the toolbar

Tap this area to go
to the next page

◂ Tap this area to go to
the previous page

An alternate way to navigate pages is by swiping the screen with your finger. To advance to the next page, swipe your finger across the screen from the right to left. To return to the previous page, swipe your finger from left to right.

To select an item, simply tap it. For example, tap a book cover or title on your **Home** screen to open the book.

To switch between **Portrait** mode and **Landscape** mode:

1.  While reading, tap the top of the screen to reveal the **Reading Toolbar**.

2.  Tap the **Menu** ☰ icon, then tap **Landscape** mode (or **Portrait m**ode).

## *Managing the PagePress Settings*

When you squeeze the PagePress controls on your Voyage, the device vibrates. You can turn this feature on and off and adjust the sensitivity.

1.  Tap the Menu ☰ icon, then tap **Settings**.

2.  Tap **Reading Options**, then tap **PagePress**. Choose an option in the menu that appears. Turn PagePress controls **On** or **Off**.

    •  Set the **Feedback Settings** to **Low**, **Medium** or **High**. Tap **Off** to turn off feedback.

- When PagePress is turned off, you can turn from page to page by tapping the left or right side of the screen, or swiping your finger across the screen in either direction.

- **Pressure Settings** lets you adjust the amount of force required to turn a page. Choose among **Low**, **Medium** or **High**.

## *Navigating Comics and Graphic Novels*

Some graphic novels and comics are specially formatted for viewing on Kindles, supporting features such as **Kindle Panel View**, **Kindle Text Pop-Up**, and zooming in on and panning across images and tables.

- View one panel at a time:

  1. Double-tap the page to launch **Panel View**.

  2. Tap the right side of the screen to advance to the next panel. Tap the left side of the screen to view the previous panel.

  3. Double-tap the panel to exit **Panel View**.

- Zoom in or pan across images and tables:

  1. Double-tap the image or table.

  2. Pinch outward to zoom in, or press and drag to pan across the image or table.

  3. Pinch inward to zoom out, or tap the **X** in the upper-right corner of the image to continue reading.

## *Navigating with Toolbars*

Depending on what content you're viewing at the moment, you can access three navigation toolbars—the **standard** toolbar, **reading** toolbar, and **reading navigation** toolbar.

Tap the top of your screen to display a toolbar. Below is a picture of the **Standard** toolbar.

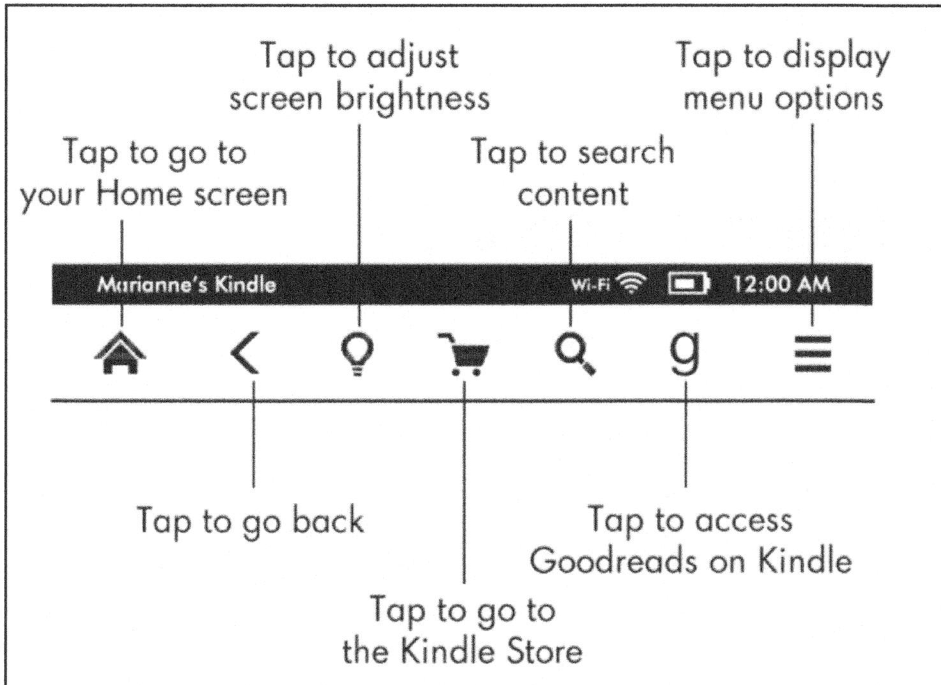


**Above: The Standard toolbar appears at the top of the screen when you click the "Home" icon.**

The options which appear in the **Standard** toolbar are:

**Home**: Tap ⌂ to go to the **Home** screen, where you'll see a list of the books and other content stored on your Voyage.

**Back:** Tap ‹ to retrace your steps. For example, if you tap a link in the book and the web page opens, tap **Back** to return to the book.

**Brightness :** Tap ⚲ to adjust the brightness of your display.

**Kindle Store:** The cart 🛒 icon links to Amazon's Kindle bookstore. You must have a wireless connection to access the store.

**Search:** Tap the **magnifying glass** 🔍 icon to display a search box, enabling you to search your books.

**Goodreads:** The **Goodreads** g icon provides access to Goodreads, a community for book lovers where you can rate and share book recommendations.

**Menu:** The **menu** ≡ icon displays a list of options including the **Kindle store**, **View special offers**, **sync and check for items**, and **Settings**.

While you're reading a book, if you tap the top of the screen, the **Reading** toolbar is displayed, as pictured below:

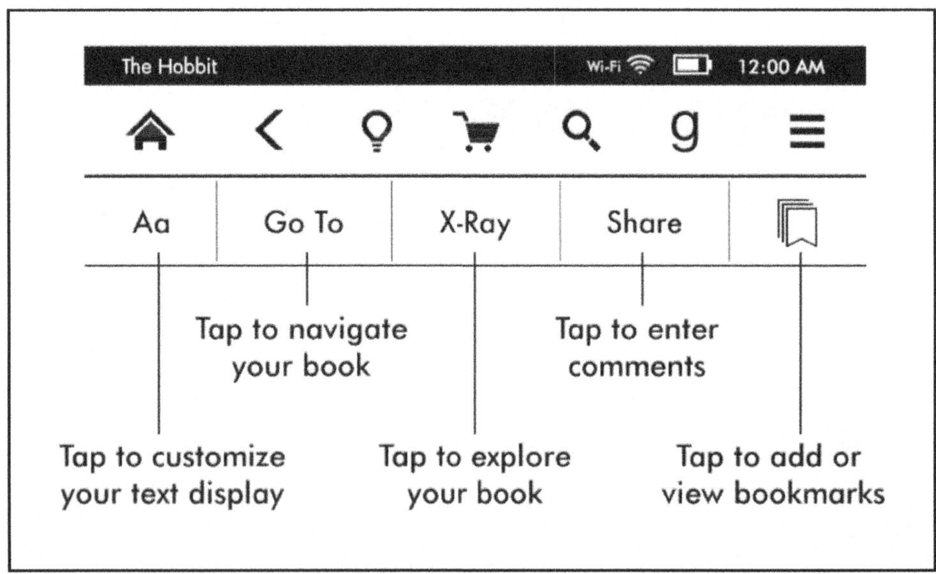


**Above: The Reading toolbar appears when you tap the top of the screen while reading a document.**

The Reading Toolbar options include:

**Text (Aa):** Tap to display font and text options. Adjust the font size, typeface, publisher font, line spacing, and margins.

**Go To:** Opens navigation tabs including **Contents** (show chapter headings) and **Notes** (to view your notes and highlights, and public notes and highlights).

**X-Ray:** Explore the book's "skeleton." You'll see all passages in a book mentioning specific ideas, characters, historical figures, places or topics. If X-Ray isn't enabled for the book you're viewing, the button is disabled.

**Share:** Tap to share your thoughts with other readers.

**Bookmark:** Add or delete a bookmark on the current page. View prevously added bookmarks.

When reading, swipe up from the bottom of the page to display the **reading navigation** toolbar, which provides a graphic illustration of your progress in a book and lets you quickly jump ahead to preview upcoming sections. The toolbar is pictured below:

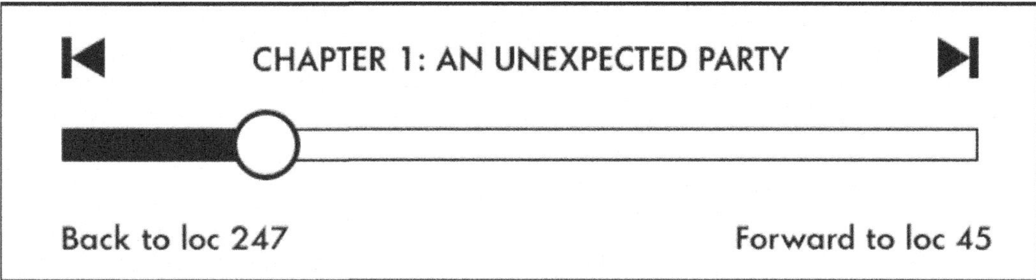



**Above: The reading navigation toolbar gives a visual indication of how far along in a document you are.**

## Periodical Toolbar

When you're reading a magazine or newspaper, you'll see a special toolbar when you tap the top of the screen.

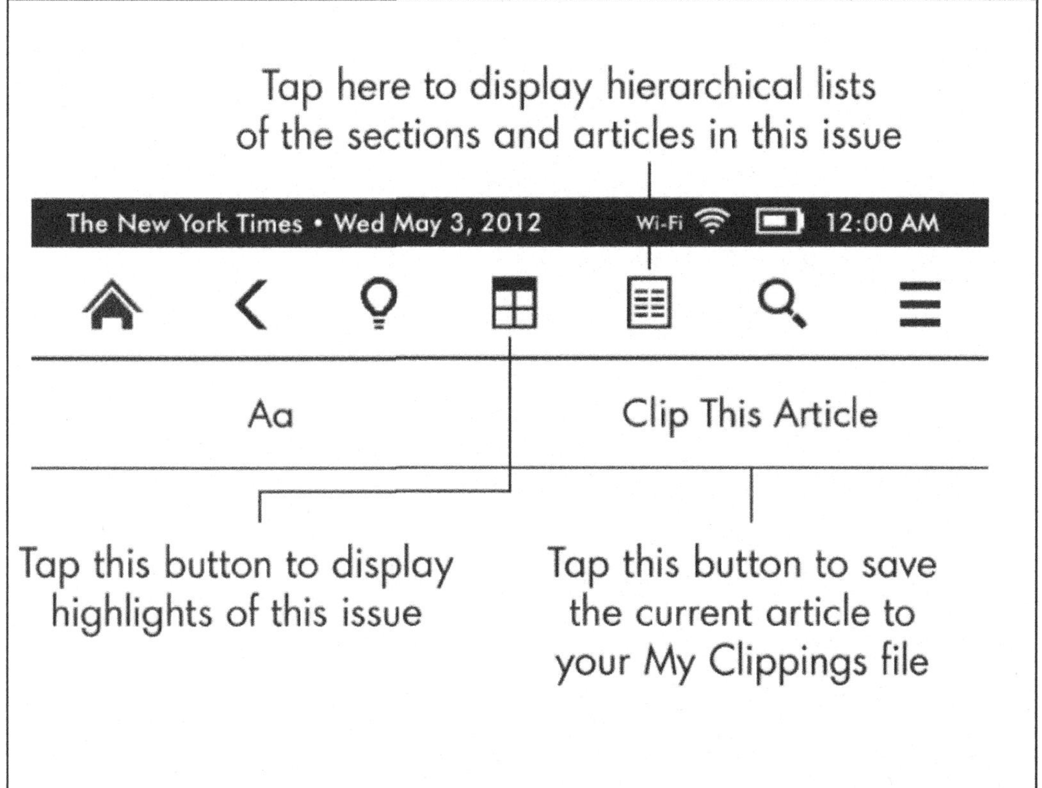



**Above: The Periodical toolbar appears when you tap the top of the screen while reading a newspaper or magazine.**

**Periodical Home:** Tap to display highlights of the issue you're reading.

**Sections and Articles:** Tap to see a hierarchical list of sections and articles.

Another toolbar is available for periodicals on the article detail page. The options are:

**Text (Aa):** Tap to display font and text options.

**Clip This Article:** Tap to clip an article to your **My Clippings** file. The file, located on your **Home** screen, stores your notes, bookmarks, highlights, and clipped articles.

## Using the On-screen Keyboard

When you tap the **Search** icon or initiate other actions requiring you to type text, the on-screen keyboard appears at the bottom of the screen, as shown below.

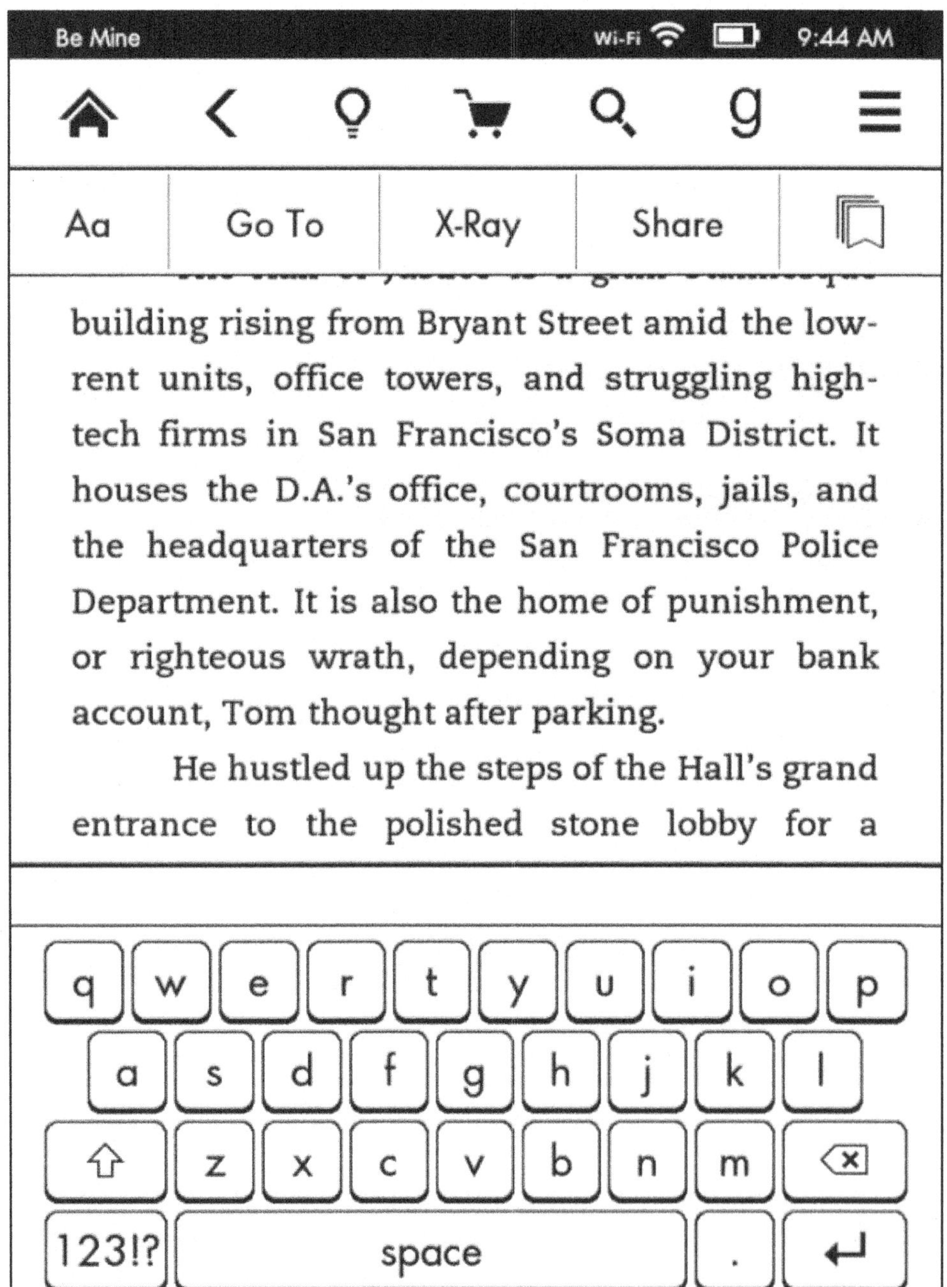


**Above: The on-screen keyboard appears when you're required to enter text.**

To enter numbers or symbols, tap the **numbers** key [123!?]. Tap the **ABC** key to return to the regular keyboard. Tap the shift key [⇧] to enter capital letters.

If you have a smartphone or other touch-screen device, you're probably already familiar with the basics of a touch-screen keyboard. If you're not, the learning curve shouldn't be too steep, but there may be some frustration initially. Here are some basic  tips to keep in mind.

- It's easier to type accurately if your Voyage is in landscape mode—the keyboard is enlarged, giving you more room to type.

- Use your thumbs to type while holding the device in your hand.

## *Viewing Status Indicators*

Along the top of your **Home** screen, you'll see indicators to the status of your Voyage. You can also view these indicators within a book by tapping the top of the screen to display the toolbar.

The first three indicators we'll look at are **wireless** status indicators:

**Wi-Fi** 📶 Your Kindle has a **Wi-Fi** connection. The more bars that appear, the stronger your connection.

**3G** 📶 Your Kindle is using a **3G** cellular network. (Only the Kindle 3G model has this indicator. At times the indicator represents an EDGE or GPRS network.)

✈ Your Voyage is in **Airplane** mode and has no wireless connection.

🔋 **Battery Status.** The battery indicator shows how much power remains. While your Kindle is charging, a lightning bolt appears within the battery indicator.

⚙ **Activity indicator:** This wheel icon appears in the top left corner of your screen while the Kindle is scanning or connecting to a network, downloading new content, checking for new items, or opening a large file or web page.

🔒 **Parental Controls indicator.** This indicates you've turned on specific restrictions or a Kindle FreeTime profile is active.

## Getting Help From Amazon

If you need to contact Amazon's customer support staff, click the "Contact Us" button on the right side of any help web page, such as www.Amazon.com/help and then choose your preferred method of contact, such as "phone," "email" or "chat." Using the contact form automatically informs Amazon's staff who you are, and it saves you the trouble of having to confirm your identify.

If you'd rather phone Amazon direct, the numbers are:

U.S. and Canada: 1-866-216-1072
Spanish Support: 866-749-7538
International: 1-206-266-2992

If you'd rather phone Amazon direct, the numbers are:

U.S. and Canada: 1-866-216-1072
Spanish Support: 866-749-7538
International: 1-206-266-2992

# 2 ▶ READING A BOOK, VOYAGE STYLE

After you've established a wireless connection, you're ready to go shopping. When you purchase a book, magazine or newspaper, it automatically downloads to your Voyage. Meanwhile, the content is also stored in the Cloud—so it's available to download to other Kindle devices or reading apps registered to your account.

## Manage Your Payment Settings

All of your transactions with Amazon via the Voyage require a valid payment setting, even if you are downloading a free item. To view or change your payment setting:

1. Visit **Manage Your Content and Devices** (http://www.amazon.com/mycd ) and click **Kindle Payment Settings**.

2. Click **Edit**. This will launch the **Your Default 1-Click** payment setting page, where you can edit the settings.

3. Select your credit card information and click **Continue**. If desired, you can add a new card.

4. Enter your billing address and click **Continue**. You'll arrive at the **Kindle Payment Settings** page, where you can view your edited 1-Click payment method.

### *Shopping at the Kindle store*

To visit the Kindle store, tap the **Shop** icon.

When you're ready to purchase an item, tap the **Buy** button. (Or tap **Try Sample** to download and read the beginning of the item for free. To subscribe to a periodical, tap **Subscribe Now**.)

Tap the **Home** icon to open your new content.

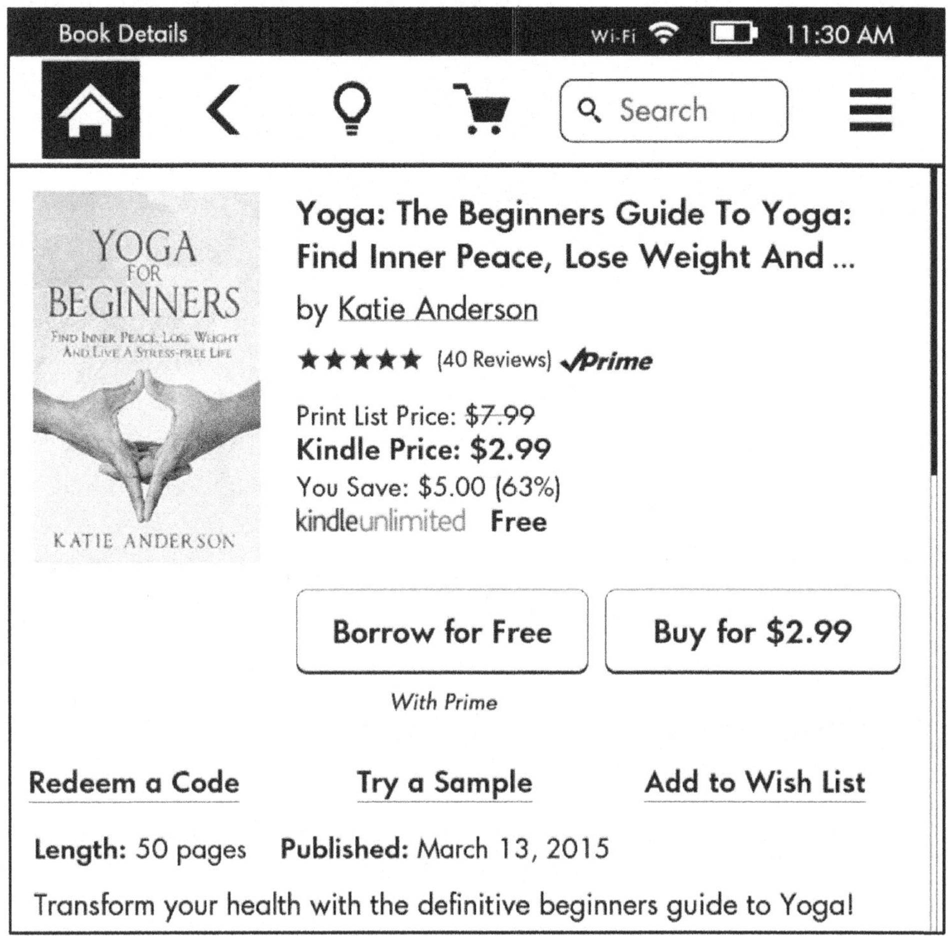


**Above: Here's a book listing in Amazon's Kindle store. From here, you can buy the book, try a sample, or add it to your wish list.**

## Accidentally Purchasing a Book

If you buy a book by mistake, you can ask Amazon for a refund within seven days of purchase.

1. Visit **Manage Your Content and Devices** at  www.amazon.com/mycd

2. Beside the title, click **Actions**, then click **Return for refund**.

## Undelivered Content

If you don't receive a book, app, video or other content after purchasing it, manually sync your device to check for pending downloads from the Amazon Cloud:

- From Home, tap the **Menu** icon, then tap **Sync & Check** for items. Titles pending delivery to your Kindle should begin downloading.

- If you still don't receive purchased content, check to ensure you have a wireless connection. Also, double-check to ensure your 1-Click payment method is still valid:

    1. Visit **Manage Your Content and Devices** at http://www.amazon.com/mycd

    2. Under **Your Kindle Account**, click **Kindle Payment Settings**.

    3. Under **Your Default 1-Click Payment Method**, click **Edit** to review or edit your 1-Click payment settings.

## *View Your Reading Progress*

With a paper-bound book, you have a simple reference point to judge your progress. By looking at the stack of pages, it's easy to see if you're halfway through a book, three-quarters of the way through, or somewhere in between. With Kindle books, you have three reference points—the number of "pages" read, the percentage of a book read, or the amount of time left in the chapter or book.

**Location numbers** – These are the digital equivalent of physical page numbers, and provide a way to easily reference a place in your reading material regardless of font size. The location displayed in a Kindle book is specific to the Kindle format and doesn't match the page number of printed editions.

**Page numbers** – These correspond to a book's printed edition. Not all Kindle books include page numbers. Because the font size and other elements are variable, it's possible to view more than one page (or less than a full page) on your screen at one time.

**Time to Read** – This feature uses your reading speed to calculate how much time is left before you finish your chapter or book.

While reading, tap the lower left corner of the screen to toggle between:

- Time left in chapter

- Time left in book

- Location numbers

- Page numbers (if available)

Another way to access your Reading Progress:

1. While reading, tap the top of the screen to show the reading toolbar.

2. Tap the **Menu** ≡ icon, then tap **Reading Progress**.

Select the tracking option you want displayed at the bottom of your screen:

- **Location in book**

- **Page in book** (if available)

- **Time left in chapter**

- **Time left in book**

- **None**

## *Jump to Other Locations in a Book*

While reading, you can use **Page Flip** to skim other pages or sections and quickly jump back and forth without losing your place.

1. Tap the top of the screen to show the reading toolbar, then tap the bottom of the screen to launch a preview window and progress bar.

2. To view other locations in the book through the preview window:

   - Swipe within the window, or tap the left or right arrows in the window.

   - Press and drag the circle left or right in the progress bar at the bottom.

   - Tap the left or right arrows at the bottom.

3. In the preview window, tap the page to go to that location in the book, or tap **X** in the top-right corner to return to your current place in the book.

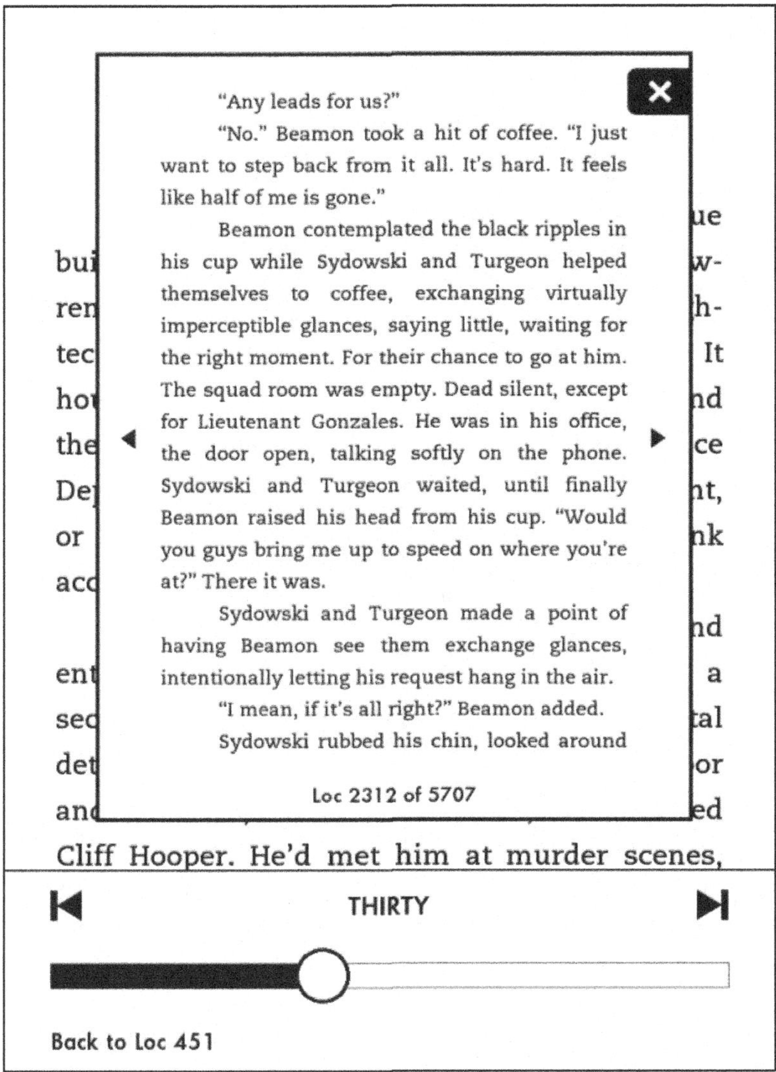

**Above: Use the progress bar and preview window to glance at another location in a book.**

## *Change Fonts, Line Spacing or Margins*

You can change the fonts, font size, line spacing, or margins displayed for a Kindle book.

1. While reading, tap the top of your screen to display the reading toolbar, then tap **Aa**.

2. Change the text display for your book:

   - Font size – Select the size of the text.

   - Font type – Select the typeface of the text.

3. Set the line spacing and margins:

   - Line spacing – Select the amount of blank space to appear above and below each line.

   - Margins – Select the amount of space to appear on the left and right edges of each page.

4. Tap the **X** in the top-right corner to return to reading.

**Display Settings**  ✕

Aa  Aa  Aa  **Aa** Aa Aa Aa Aa

○ Baskerville          ○ Futura

○ Caecilia             ○ Helvetica

○ Caecilia Condensed   ⊙ Palatino

○ Publisher Font

**Line spacing**          **Margins**

**Above: From the reading toolbar, tap Aa to display options for changing fonts, line spacing or margins.**

The text size of menus and other screens is fixed; you can't modify them. Likewise, you can't change the text appearance of PDF documents.

## Manage Your Library

After you've accumulated dozens—or perhaps hundreds—of digital items, keeping track of it all might seem daunting. Fortunately, Amazon has a system that makes it simple. By visiting the **Manage Your Content and Devices** web page at www.amazon.com/mycd, you can locate and deliver items from your Kindle Library to your Kindle devices or reading apps.

### *Deliver Items to Your Kindle*

1. Visit **Manage Your Content and Devices** at www.amazon.com/mycd

2. Under **Your Content**, locate the item you want to deliver. Click on the box under the **Select** heading to mark the item with a checkmark.

3. Click the box under the **Actions** heading. In the pop-up box, check **Deliver.**

4.  Select your Voyage or other device from the drop-down menu.

5.  Click **Deliver**. Your book or other content will be sent to your Voyage or reading app.

6.  On your Kindle Voyage, go to the **Home** screen, and then tap the **On Device** tab to view and open the title.

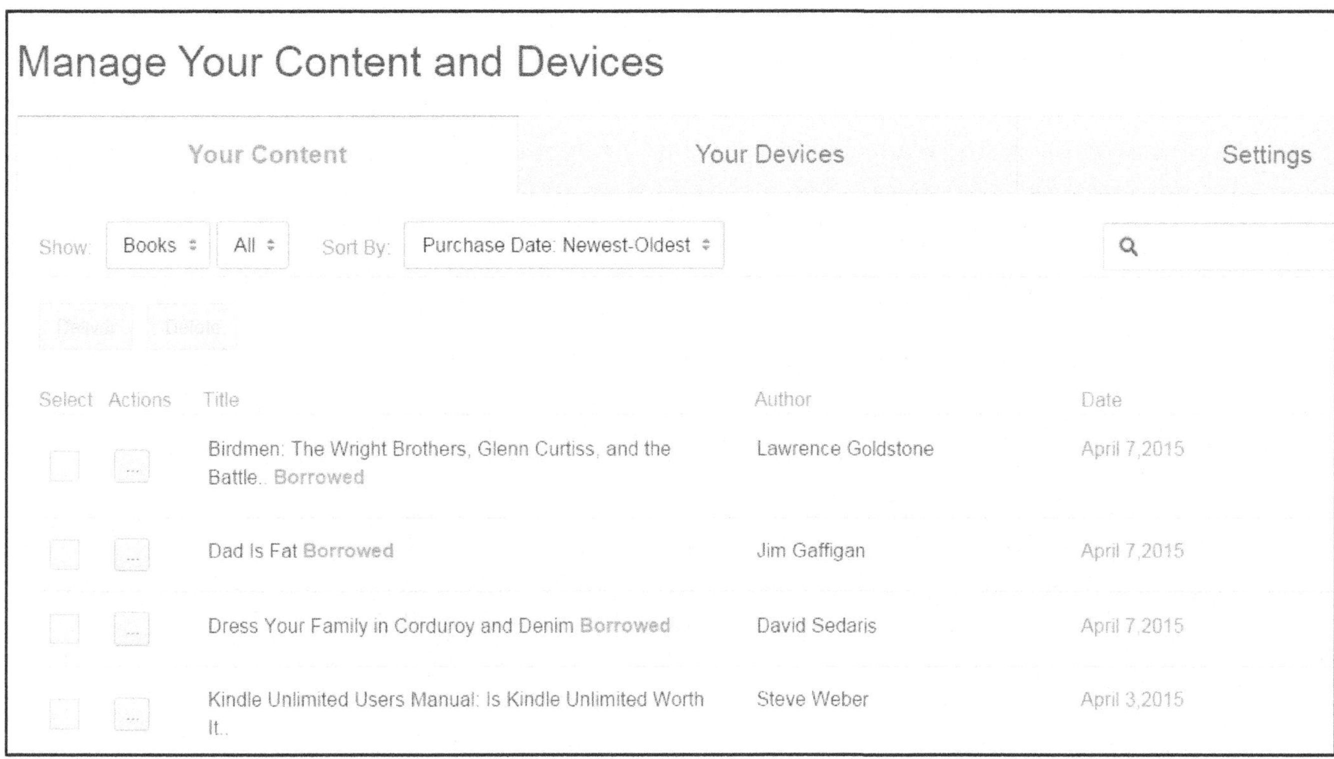

Above: The "Manage Your Content and Devices" web page at www.amazon.com/mycd

## Family Library

Lots of families have more than one Kindle in the household. The "easy" way to share Kindle books with family members is to register multiple devices with the same Amazon email address. For example, in my household, each Kindle device—mine, my wife's, our young daughter's—is registered to my Amazon email address. My account is used for all Kindle purchases, so each book we buy is automatically shared among all our Kindles. It's convenient, but the adults in the household must take care not to purchase content that is inappropriate for youngsters.

Another way to share Kindle books is to use the **Family Library** feature. Family Library adds more control—books may still be shared, but certain content may remain private. For example, both spouses can link their two Amazon accounts on their Kindles, enabling them to share books. Meanwhile, those two folks can jointly supervise and control the accounts of as many as four children.

The only slight drawback with Family Library is that it takes some time to set up. For more details, visit www.bit.ly/FamilyLibrary.

## *Sync Your Voyage*

Amazon's **Whispersync** feature enables you to synchronize all your Kindle content to all your devices and Kindle apps, including your books, audiobooks, personal documents, games, and Amazon Instant Video. For example, if you stop reading a book on your Voyage at the end of chapter one, the book will automatically open at the same point on all of your other Kindle devices and apps. Whispersync also makes your annotations available to all your devices, including bookmarks, highlights and notes.

Whispersync is enabled by default. To change the setting:

1. Visit **Manage Your Content and Devices** at www.amazon.com/mycd

2. Under **Your Kindle Account**, click **Manage Your Devices**.

3. Under **Device Synchronization** (Whispersync Settings), tap the button for **Whispersync Device Synchronization** (on or off).

Occasionally you'll want to "sync" your Voyage, which can serve two functions for you: First, you'll prompt your Voyage to check for and download any awaiting items. Secondly, it syncs items you might be reading on other Kindle devices or apps—so you can automatically resume reading at the place you left off, even if you switch devices.

- From Home, tap the **Menu** ☰ icon, then tap **Sync & Check for Items**. Titles that were delivered to your Kindle—and saved bookmarks and annotations—should begin downloading to your Voyage.

- While reading, tap the **Menu** ☰ icon, then tap **Sync to the Furthest Page Read**. When you're finished reading, make it a habit to return to the **Home** screen, which records your reading progress and prevents syncing errors.

## Use Bookmarks, Highlights and Notes

You can add, view or remove bookmarks within Kindle books or personal documents.

- Add a bookmark:

1.  Tap the top-right corner of the screen to show the **Bookmark** icon, then tap + and the Bookmark icon will turn black .

- View your bookmarks:

    1.  Tap the top-right corner of the screen to show the Bookmark icon. A list of your bookmarks appears.

- Tap a bookmark in the list to preview that location in the book. Tap the preview window to jump to that location in the book.

- Remove a bookmark:

    1.  Tap the top-right corner of the screen to show the **Bookmark** icon.

    2.  Tap a bookmark in the list, then tap **X** to delete that bookmark.

## Add, View or Remote Highlights

You can add, view or remove highlights within a Kindle book or personal document.

- **Highlight a word:** Press and hold the word, tap **More**, then tap **Highlight**.

- **Highlight a phrase:** Press and drag to highlight the desired passage, then tap **Highlight**.

- **Highlight multiple pages:** Press and drag to highlight the desired text to the bottom-right corner of the page. The page will turn and the highlight will automatically continue to the first period on the next page. You can drag the handle at the start or end of the highlighted text to refine your selection.

- **Remove a highlight:** Press and hold a word in the highlighted area, tap **More**, and then tap **Delete**.

- **View your highlights:**

    1.  Tap the top of the screen to display the reading toolbar, tap **Go To**, then tap the **Notes** tab.

    2.  Tap the **Yours** tab to view notes and highlights you've created. Tap a note or highlight to jump to that location in the book.

## Add, View, Edit or Remove Notes

You can add, view, edit or remove notes within a Kindle book or personal document.

- Add a note:

1. Press and hold a word or press and drag to highlight the desired text. If you selected a word, tap **More**, tap **Add Note**, and then type your desired text. If you selected a phrase, tap **Add Note**, then type your text.

2. Tap **Save** to create your note.

- Edit a note:

   1. Tap the number where the note appears, then tap **Edit Note**.

   2. Make your chnages, then tap **Save**.

- Remove a Note:

   1. Tap the number where the note appears, then tap **More**.

   2. Tap **Delete Note**.

- View your notes:

   1. Tap the top of the screen to display the reading toolbar, tap the **Menu** ≡ icon, then then tap **Notes**.

   2. Tap **Yours** to view notes and highlights you've created. Tap a note or highlight to jump to that location in the book.

## View Popular Highlights and Public Notes

Amazon displays Popular Highlights and Public Notes by combining input from all Kindle users and identifying the passages with the most highlights and notes.

- To turn on Popular Highlights or Public Notes:

   1. While reading, tap the top of the screen to show the reading toolbar.

   2. Tap the **Menu** ≡ icon and then tap **Settings**.

   3. Tap **Reading Options** and then tap **Notes & Highlights**.

   4. Beside **Popular Highlights** or **Public Notes**, tap **Off**. The switch moves to the **On** position. When you resume reading, frequently selected highlights will appear as you read.

- To view a list of Popular Highlights or Public Notes:

   1. While reading, tap the top of your screen to display the reading toolbar.

   2. Tap **Go To**, then tap the **Notes** tab.

# 3 ▶ FEED YOUR KINDLE WITH FREE CONTENT

Finding free content for your Voyage isn't difficult. In fact, you'll find that there are plenty of sites out there—including Amazon itself—offering free content of one type or another. These sites may offer a variety of different types of content, from video to audio to books. While you're exploring them, you'll want to avoid illegal pirate sites.

Now, for the good news: There is actually a ton of free content out there that you can download for your Voyage and, better yet, it's entirely legal.

## Public Domain Books

Many older popular books are no longer under copyright, and so they're in the "Public Domain" and usually available free in e-book formats. For instance, the works of Edgar Allen Poe, Mary Shelly, Jane Austin and Charlotte Bronte were written so long ago, nobody owns the rights anymore. There is a caveat here, however.

If you buy a specific publisher's edition of a public domain work, that edition is copyrighted. The edition likely has unique material in it that does fall under the copyright protection of the publisher and, therefore, it cannot be reproduced in full. To put it in shorthand terms: You can reproduce *The Raven* all you want, but you cannot reproduce a copyrighted analysis of *The Raven* included in a printing of the poem.

There are several sites that offer public domain books. The most well-known is likely Project Gutenberg, located at www.gutenberg.org

## *Exploring Project Gutenberg*

The illustration above shows the Project Gutenberg homepage. The left navigation menu gives you access to the site's entire book catalog. You can choose to **Search Catalog**, **Browse Catalog** or you can view **Book Categories**.

Let's search for a well-known suspense story, *The Turn of the Screw* by Henry James. Here is the result from Project Gutenberg:

Above: Search results for *Turn of the Screw* at Project Gutenberg.

Notice that, on the right of the page, there are two results listed. The first result is a link to the e-book version. The second result is a link to the audio version of the story. (Project Gutenberg has a lot of audio books that are public domain and that are read by volunteers. If you want to stock up on audio books for a long trip, this is a good place to do it!)

Let's click on the link to the e-book version of *The Turn of the Screw*.

**Above: The e-book versions of** *The Turn of the Screw*

Project Gutenberg will typically offer books in a variety of formats. Notice that there are HTML, EPUB, Kindle, PLocker, QiOO Mobile and Plain Text versions of this e-book.

Simply click on the link to download the e-book and save it to your computer. You can either transfer the book to your Voyage manually or you can do so through your Calibre library, which will allow you to assign it a cover and other metadata, as I did with *The Raven*.

## *Public Domain Books on Amazon*

Like Project Gutenberg, Amazon offers thousands of classic Public Domain works absolutely free. These books remain free all year long, and many of them are the same texts available through Project Gutenberg.

Let's do a search for "Bronte" on Amazon.com. This will bring up books by the Bronte sisters. On the right side of the web page, select **Price—Low to High** and the free public domain books will appear.

TIP: Many rare and out-of-print books are now available as e-books from several different sites. If you've been searching for a book that means a lot to you to own—maybe something from your childhood or with similar sentimental value—be sure to check Project Gutenberg and Amazon. It may well be available on one of these sites.

Even though a particular book might be "free," you'll still need a 1-Click payment method at Amazon to download them. You'll get a receipt in your email that will show the purchase but nothing will show up on your credit card or bank statement.

## Lend or Borrow Kindle Books

Remember the days when you'd loan your paperback books to friends, and (depending on the friend) rarely see the book again? Well, a great feature of lending books via your Kindle is that all your books will actually be returned—there's no way around it. Loans are capped at 14 days by Amazon's system.

Not all Kindle books are eligible for lending—the publisher has to agree to the program. When you're shopping for Kindle books nowadays, you'll see a notation—whether lending is **enabled** or not—in the **Product Details** of the book's listing on Amazon.

**TIP:** Remember, you can loan Kindle books to virtually anyone with an email address, regardless of whether they have a Kindle device. They can read the book on a free Kindle reading app on their computer or smartphone. Kindle reading apps are available free for practically every type of computer, smartphone, and other digital gadgets.

You're allowed to lend Kindle books only once per title. During the loan period, you won't have access to the book.

Visit the Kindle store and locate the product page for the book.

From the product page, click **Loan this book**.

Enter the borrower's email address (their regular email address, not a Kindle address) and an optional personal message.

Click **Send Now**.

You can also loan Kindle books from the **Manage Your Content and Devices** page at www.amazon.com/mycd . In the **Actions** menu, select **Loan this title**. Borrowers can return loaned books via **Manage Your Content and Devices**.

## Borrow Books From the Kindle Owner's Lending Library

Amazon Prime members can borrow one book per month from the Kindle Owner's Lending Library with no due dates. Not all books are eligible for borrowing.

1.  Tap the top of the screen to reveal the toolbar, then tap the **Kindle Store** icon.

2.  Near the top-right corner of the screen, tap **All Categories**.

3.  Tap **Kindle Owners' Lending Library**.

Eligible titles display the Prime badge: **✓Prime**

Amazon Prime charges an annual fee and offers many benefits. If you're not a member and like the idea of the Lending Library, you may want to look into Prime's offerings, which include free videos and free two-day shipping on eligible products.  See http://bit.ly/amazonPrime

## Borrow Books From a Public Library

You can borrow Kindle books from the websites of local libraries and have them sent to your Kindle or reading app. About 11,000 U.S. libraries offer Kindle books. Just like regular library books, Kindle books may be loaned for a specific period of time. Since only one copy of a Kindle book may be loaned at one time, there might be a waiting period before you can borrow a popular title.

Confirm whether your library branch carries Kindle books. Visit your library's website or visit Overdrive, the company that handles library Kindle lending at www.search.overdrive.com

Obtain a library card and PIN from your local library.

Search for Kindle books at your library's website.

At checkout, sign into your Amazon account, and select your Kindle device.

Your Kindle should receive the book automatically. If not, sync your device manually.

Amazon sends a courtesy email to remind you three days before the book is due, and another message after the loan period ends. To return the book before the loan period ends, visit **Manage Your Content and Devices** at www.amazon.com/mycd . Click **Actions**, then **Return This Book**.

## A Whole New Calibre of Reading Material

Amazon benefits mightily from consumer loyalty. By linking their device so strongly to the AZW and MOBI formats they use, they make the average user assume they can only read e-books that are bought directly from Amazon. Fortunately, you actually can read any e-book format you want, thanks to a great program called Calibre, a program that runs on Windows or Mac desktop computers. Calibre can find all sorts of valuable non-Amazon content and format it and deliver it to your Kindle.

Calibre is free, it's stable and, to put it in the most direct terms, it's awesome—it can deliver you hundreds of dollars' worth of newspaper, magazine and book content every day, 365 days a year. The only challenge is finding the time to read that gusher of great content you're piping to your Voyage.

Let's jump right in and download the Calibre application to your computer. I have been using the program, along with thousands of others, for the past three years. The best things in life are free, and believe me, Calibre is one of them.

1.  Go to www.calibre-ebook.com and select **Download Calibre**.

2.  Open the downloaded program to install the package once it's completed.

3.  On your first run, you'll get the **Welcome Wizard**. This is designed to help you set up your libraries and to import your books, as well as to help you select the correct device!

4.  The first screen will set your Calibre Library directory. The default choice is a good one. On the next screen, you'll have to choose your device. Choose your Voyage, of course.

This sets the program up so that it knows to look for your Kindle when you click the Send to Device icon.

When you have the program installed, launch it, and study the interface for a moment. This program is capable of doing many things; even offering you a way to shop for content across a number of different stores. What we'll concern ourselves with first, however, is opening up new sources of literature by using the features built into this program that allow you to convert books from other formats into ones that your Amazon Kindle can read.

## *All the News You Can Eat, and Calibre Picks Up the Check*

Okay, I'll admit it. I'm a book nut. But I have an even bigger problem. I'm addicted to newspapers, too. I was a "news junkie" before anyone ever heard of such a thing. Twenty-five years ago, I paid about $75 a month to have three different newspapers dropped at my doorstep every morning—my local paper, the *Wall Street Journal*, and the *New York Times*.

Now, since I discovered Calibre, I've been reading six newspapers a day—plus bunch of blogs and magazines like *Newsweek* and *Time*—and it doesn't cost me one red cent. The *Washington Post*. The *New York Post*. And, if I still have time, I can read the *Onion* and a couple others—just to get my humor fix. Your local newspaper is probably available, too. Calibre downloads the content they post on their websites, and sends it, nicely formatted, to your Kindle. The only cost is the few minutes you'll spend setting it up once, and then it works every day. Here how to get started:

1.  Click on **Fetch News** in the menu.

2.  Select your language.

3.  Select a news source.

4.  In the next illustration, you can see that I've selected the *Washington Post.*

Note that I've opted to have it download automatically every day of the week after 6am. If you were the ultimate news junkie, you could set it to download the Associated Press news wire every 10 minutes.

Calibre has hundreds of different news sources available in a huge number of languages, you just click them and enjoy—free.

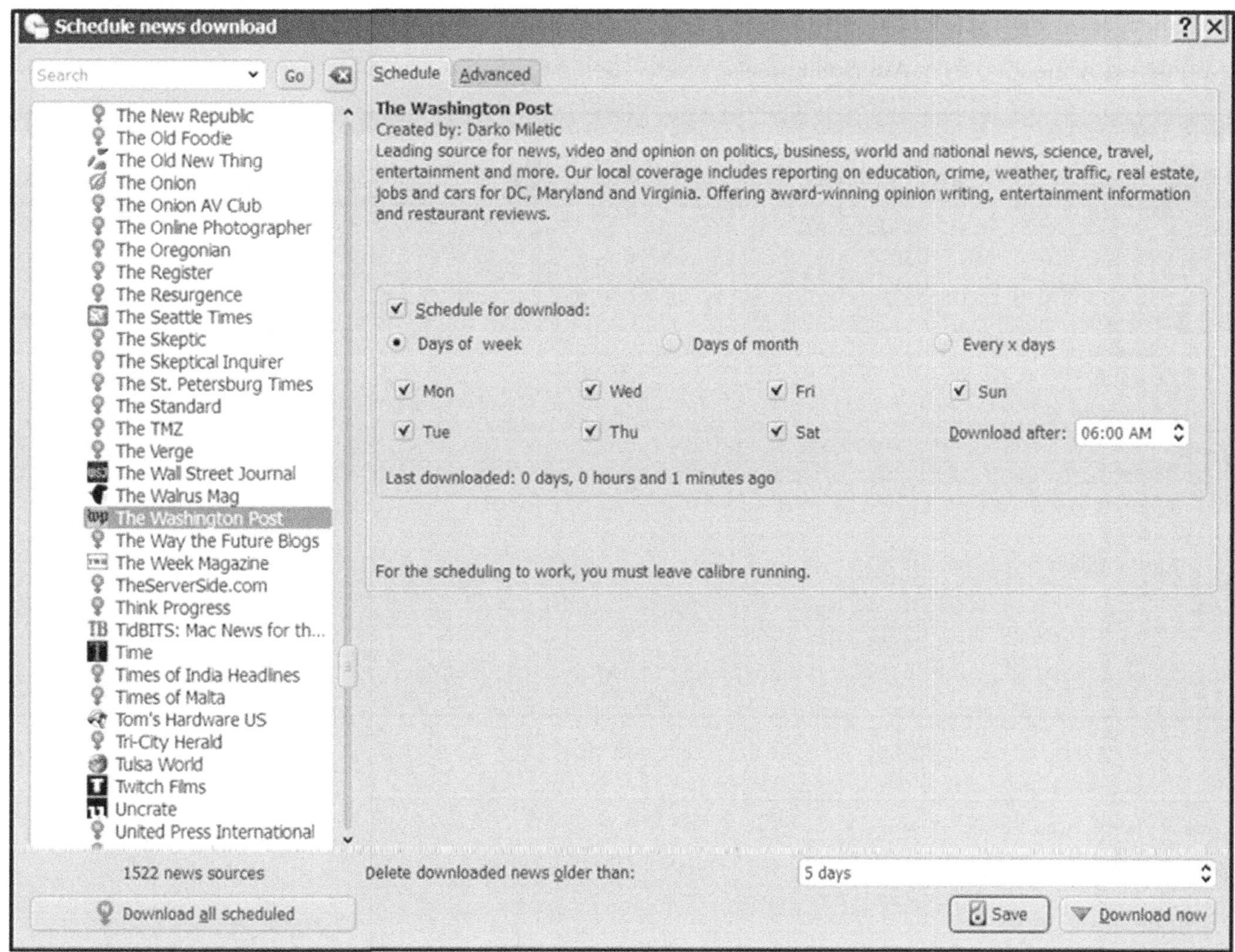

Above: Selecting the *Washington Post* news download.

Of course, you have to leave Calibre running so it automatically downloads your news sources. If you have several news sites on your list, it will take a while. Personally, I leave my computer on 24/7, and Calibre is finding news for me constantly, and feeding my Kindle. In the old days, I used to finish my three newspapers and still want more. Now, with Calibre, I don't have a prayer of skimming everything I'm tempted to read every day.

**TIP:** In this section, we're talking about downloading content for free. It sounds too good to be true, but it's totally above board. We're not stealing, we're just using the stuff that publishers are posting to their websites. Calibre simply does the work of formatting it for the Kindle and emailing it to us.

After the news site has converted, you'll be able to transfer it to your Kindle using the same interface that you use to transfer books. One of the best things about the Calibre program is that it's smart in meaningful ways. The program, for instance, will transfer newspapers to your Newsstand.

### E-Books, Calibre and the Kindle

Believe it or not, there's more to the story. In addition to newspapers and magazines, you can manage e-books—downloaded from Amazon and elsewhere—using Calibre.

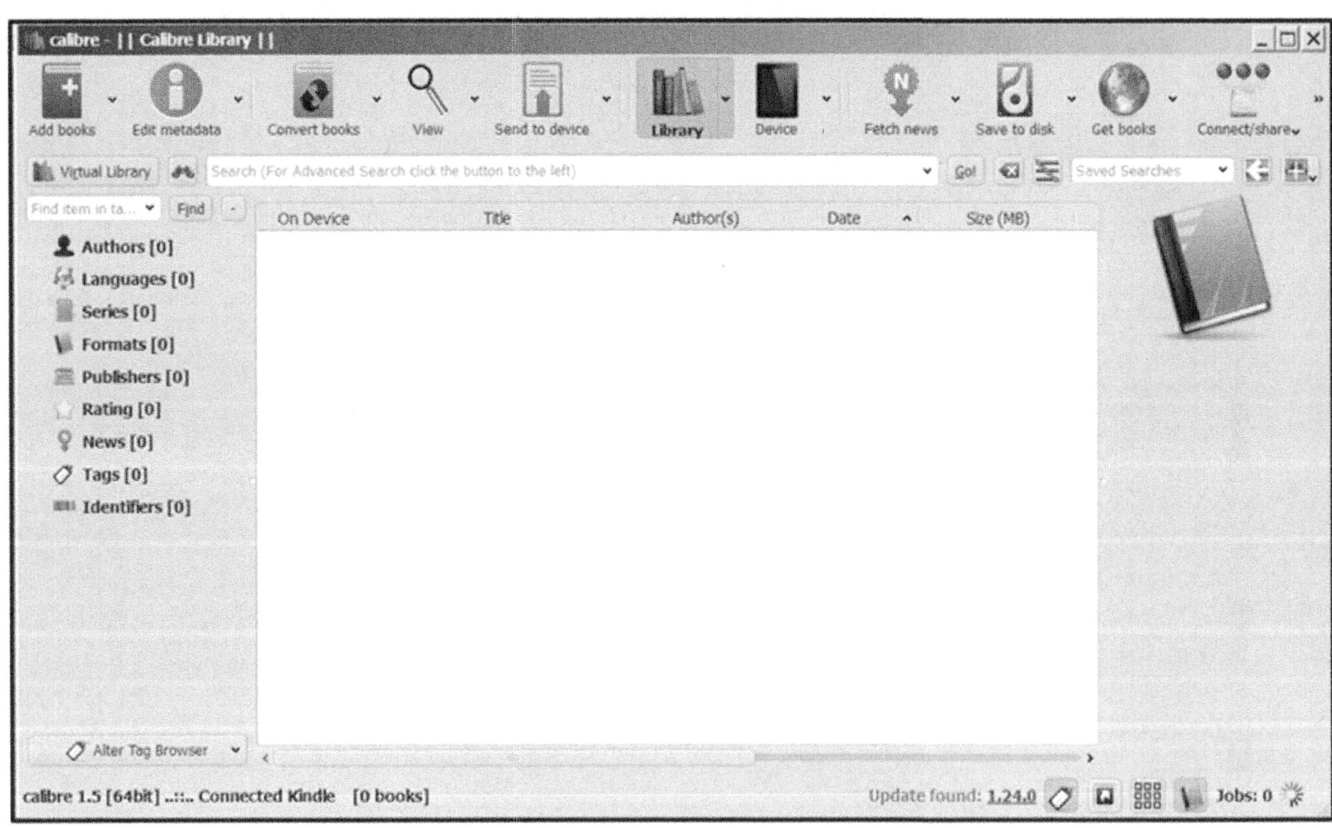

**Above: Calibre's main screen**

In the illustration above, I haven't added my e-books to the collection yet, so the middle of the screen is blank. There are many ways you can add books to your library. By default, they're sent to the **Calibre Library** folder.

The **Add Books** icon appears at the upper left. Select it, and you'll see the options shown below.

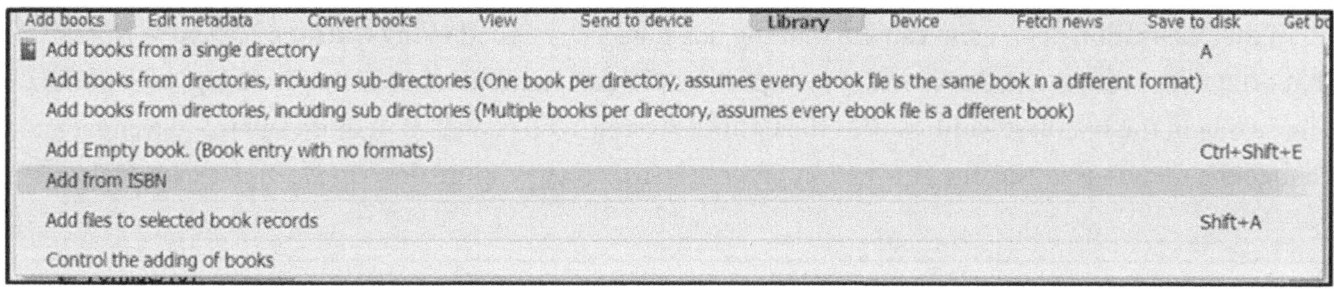


**Above: The Add Books dialog**

There are quite a few options here, but we'll concentrate adding one book to the library in a format that Kindle just doesn't like.

In this case, I'm going to add a book that's stored in the EPUB format—a popular one on many sites—that I want to read on my Voyage in the native Kindle AZW or MOBI format.

To start, click on **Add books from a single directory** and browse to the directory that you want. In the illustration below, I've chosen the book "pg1062.epub" which is actually *The Raven* by Edgar Allen Poe, which I have in the EPUB format that the Kindle will not read. I downloaded it from Project Gutenberg, a site that has plenty of public domain eBooks to choose from.

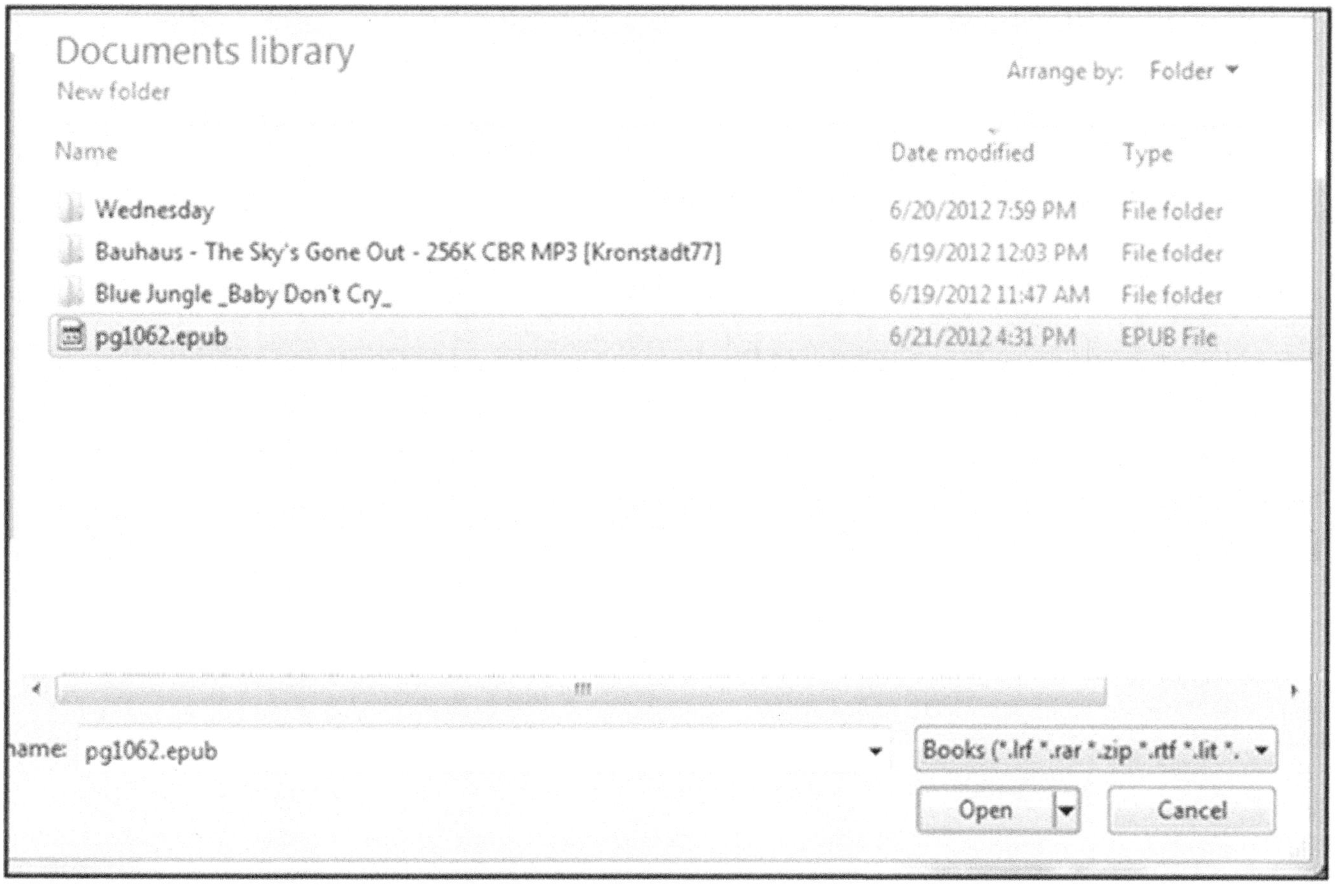

**Above: Choosing a book to import**

In the illustration below, you can see that the book has been added to my **Calibre Library**. Notice that even the cover art came over with the import, as did the description and other metatag information. This is one of the handiest features with the Calibre program. I'll change it to more suitable cover art and change the metatags during the conversion process so that they're more descriptive and accurate.

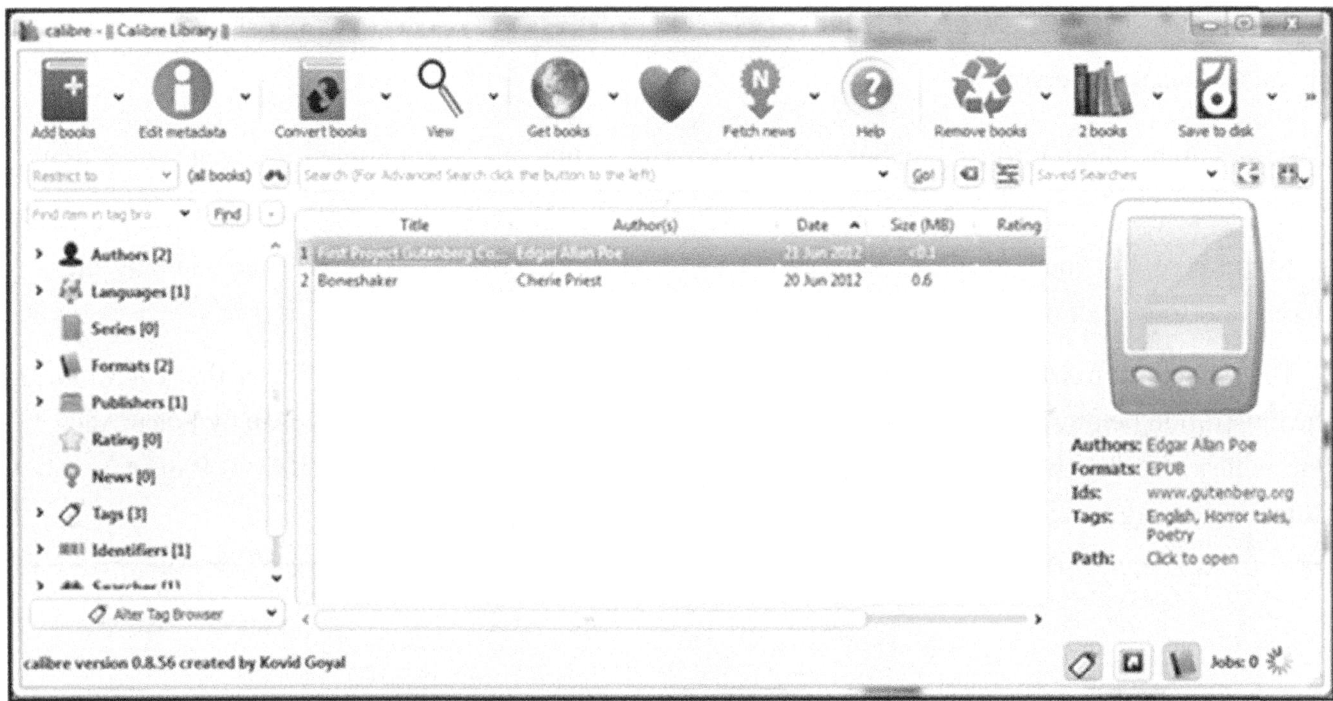

**Above: The e-book from Project Gutenberg now appears in My Library.**

Before I move this to my Voyage, I have to convert it. Fortunately, Calibre makes that very easy to do.

Highlight the title and select the **Convert Books** icon and then select **Convert individually**. The screen pictured below appears.Take a look at the options available. The **Metadata** selection controls the description, publisher credit, and other information associated with the book. Be sure to fill these out if they're not filled out already. They're important organizational tools.

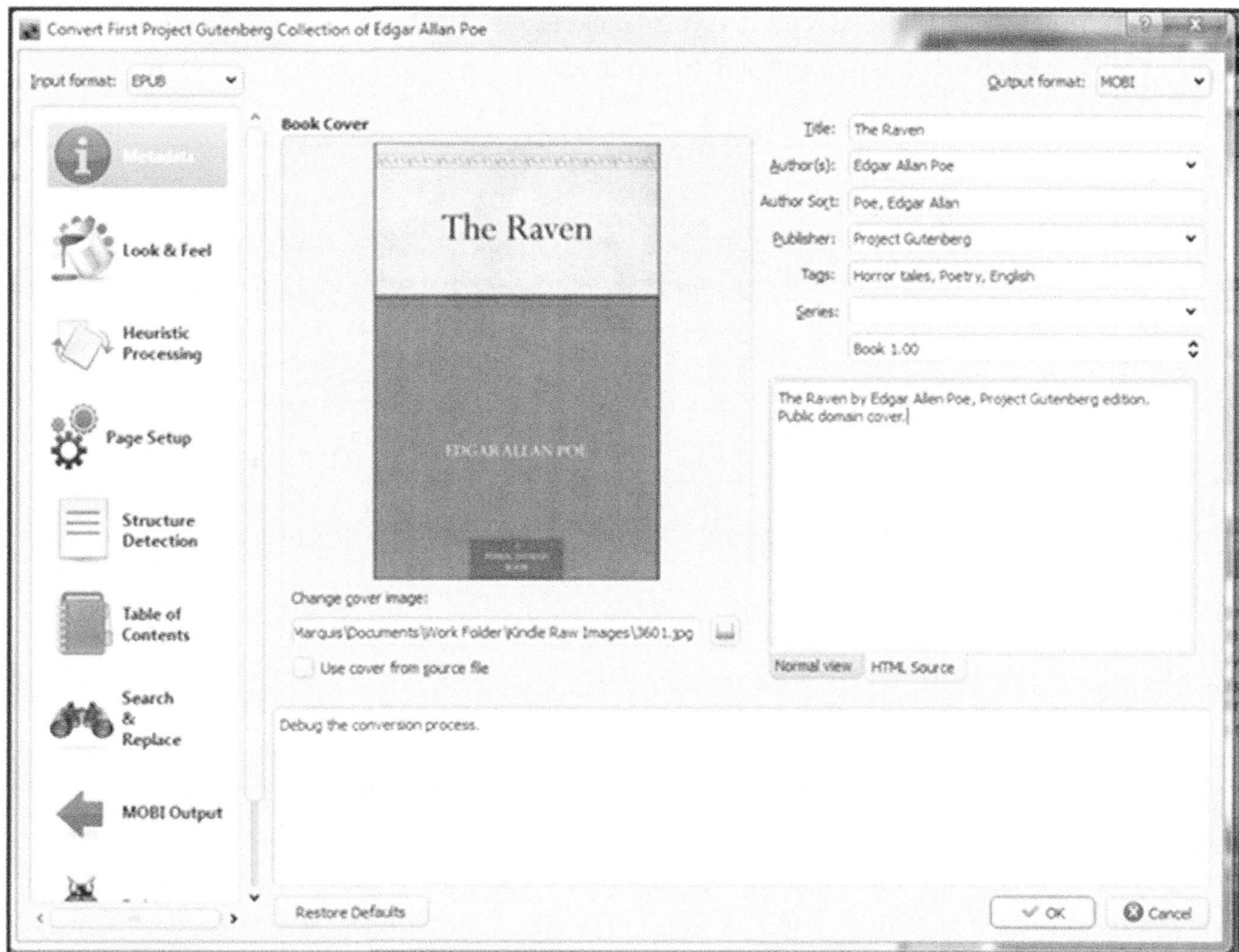

**Above: The Convert screen**

You can also change the cover image, which I've done using a public domain cover that I downloaded. I could technically use any image I wanted, however, as long as it doesn't violate anyone's copyright. You can change the **Look and Feel** of the output, which alters the text formatting, and more. One thing that Calibre does very well is give you options!

Because this book needs to be readable on the Voyage, we'll go with the MOBI format, which you can see in the upper right-most dropdown list.

**TIP:** You can convert more than one file at once, but it takes a lot of time. If you're going to do so, you might want to get a cup of coffee, order a pizza, or do something else to pass the time. If you have a slow computer, consider making your own pizza from scratch!

Now, the file has been converted to the  MOBI format, which the Voyage will be entirely happy with, but we have to move it over to the Voyage, of course.

Select, **Send to Device** from the top menu on the main screen. It will pick the device that you set up during the **Welcome Wizard**. Because the Voyage doesn't take an SD card, you can just choose **Send**

**to Main Memory** from the dropdown list. If you did have a device with additional onboard storage, Calibre would give you the option to send it to that storage.

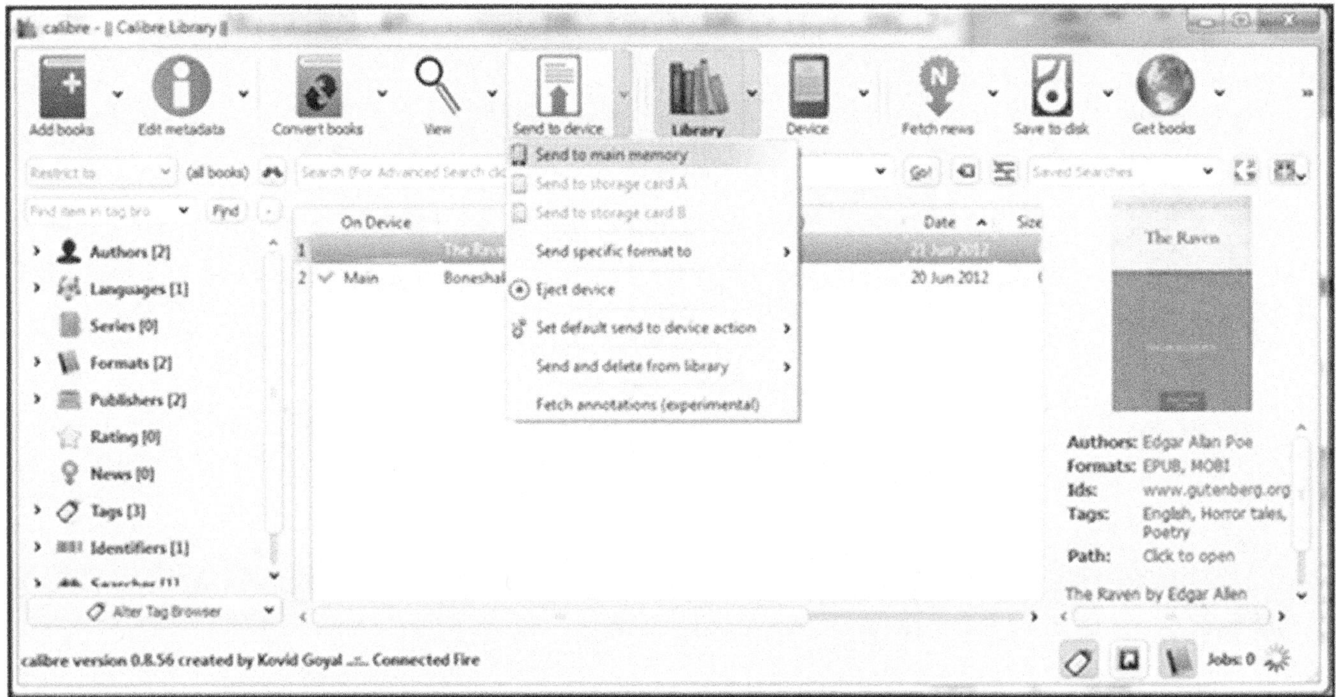

**Above: Sending the book to the Kindle.**

When the book has been sent, you'll see the listing for it under the **On Device** heading change. If I go to my **Books Library** on my Voyage and look under the titles available on my device, it shows right up.

This is only one of the functions that Calibre offers you. It's an amazingly powerful program. We'll explore it more, but be aware that this is going to be one of your most important resources for getting free books off of the Internet. The sites that offer works from the public domain sometime don't have them in a format that the Kindle reads. In the future, of course, a format may come along that is incompatible with your Kindle books. Instead of having to buy them in a new format, you'll just be able to convert them!

## Let's Go Shopping!

The Voyage makes it easy to go shopping at Amazon, and Calibre makes it easy to go shopping everywhere else. Because it can convert e-books to different formats, that means that you can hit Amazon, Barnes & Noble, Borders, Project Gutenberg or any other site out there and purchase and download books without worrying about the format.

Click on the **Get Books** icon on the top of the screen. Because I also have Cherie Priest's book *Boneshaker* on my Calibre and Kindle, I'll get the option to **Search This Author**, which I'll do.

If I wanted to, however, I could search for any book using the **Search for E-books** option. I found *The Raven* using that search function. The following search dialog will come up. Along the left hand side of the dialog, pictured below, you'll see options for which stores to search.

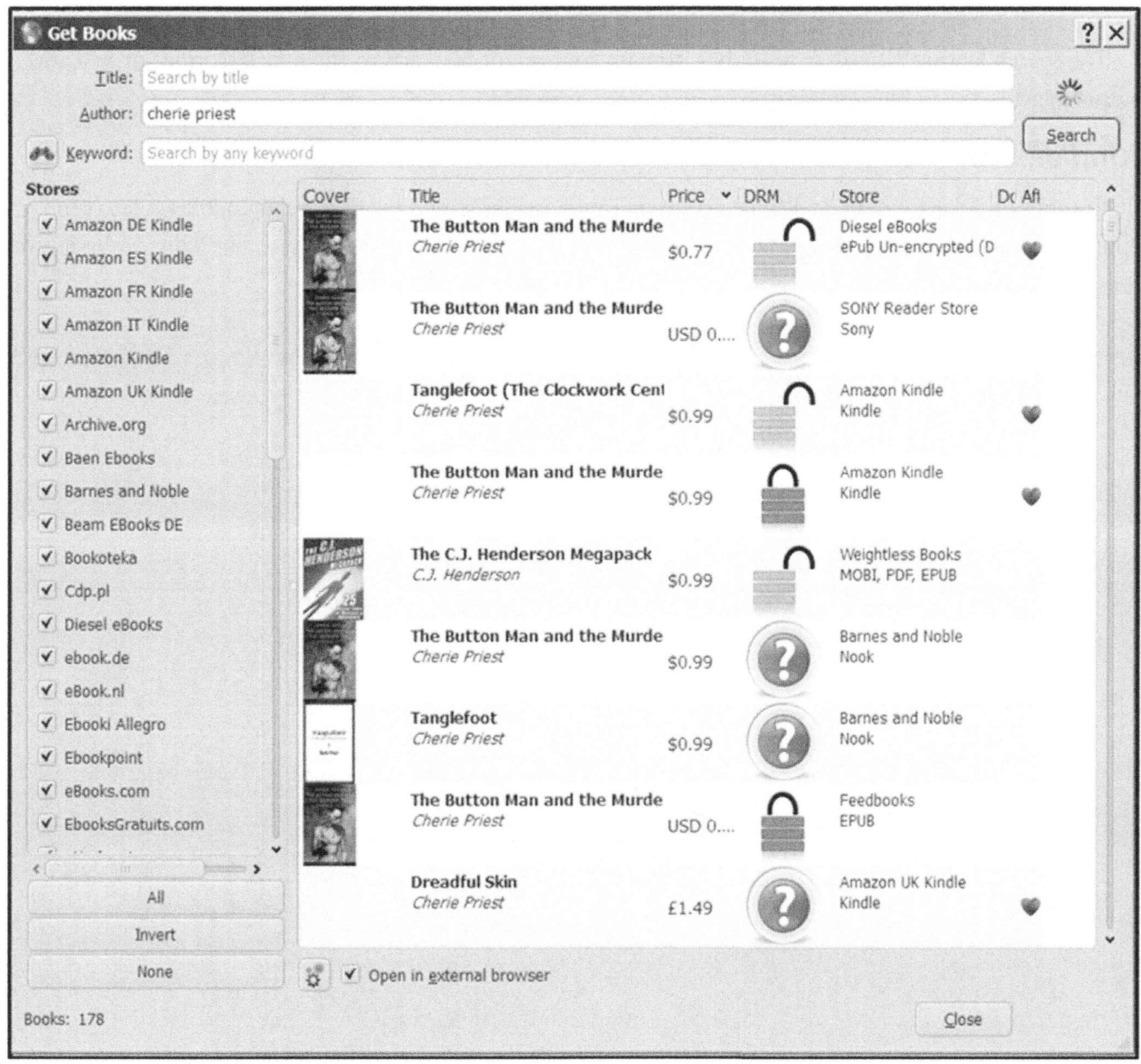

**Above: Just part of the Search Results**

Notice the locks that appear next to some of the listings. This indicates whether the book has DRM (Digital Rights Management, or copy prevention). This doesn't mean that you cannot move them from device to device, but you need an additional program to do it. It's called Adobe Digital Editions, which is also valuable for downloading books from your public library. Adobe Digital Editions allows you to authorize your e-reader, which allows the publisher to manage the DRM properly.

Clicking on any of the links in the search results will take you to the appropriate page where you can buy the book. This is an amazing feature, when you think about it. Amazon has just about everything in the way of books, of course, but there are always those books that they don't have and you can search other stores to find them if you need to.

The search feature also searches public domain sources for books. Sort the books by price or by DRM status to get to the public domain versions, if one is available.

## Kindlefeeder

Another popular third-party Kindle service is Kindlefeeder.com. Like Calibre, it enables you to send content that appears on the Internet to your Kindle via email. I suppose it's a bit easier to use at first, but doesn't have the range of Calibre. See www.kindlefeeder.com

# 4 ▶ CREATE AND  VIEW PERSONAL DOCUMENTS

One of the strongest features of the Voyage is its compact size. It's easy to tote around and, if you wish, it can often take the place of a laptop computer. If you're going to use your Kindle frequently as an e-reader or productivity tool, taking advantage of Amazon's **Personal Documents Service** is a must. Although Amazon's Kindle books use a proprietary format—you need a Kindle (or a Kindle app) to read them—you can send virtually any kind of digital document to your Kindle using the Personal Documents Service.

You can use the Personal Documents Service along with your **Send-to-Kindle** email address. The email address is usually formatted as follows: [Your Name]@Kindle.com

If you're unsure of your Send-to-Kindle address, you can review it at Amazon's **Manage Your Content and Devices** web page at www.amazon.com/mycd

## Kindle Personal Documents Service

You can send documents to your Kindle using either the **Send to Kindle** application or from an email address you've authorized (this procedure is explained in the following section). Attach the document to an email and send it to your **Send-to-Kindle email address**, which is a unique email address automatically assigned by Amazon.

Documents that you send to your Send-to-Kindle email address are stored in the Cloud and synced across all compatible Kindle devices and reading apps. The documents appear in the **Docs** library on your Kindle.

To change your Send-to-Kindle email address, visit **Manage Your Content and Devices** at www.amazon.com/mycd and click **Personal Documents Settings**.

Under **Send-to-Kindle email address**, click **Edit**.

Enter the new address, and click **Update**.

If your document needs to be converted to Kindle's .azw format, enter "convert" in the email's subject line.

## Your Approved Personal Document Email List

Your Kindle can only receive documents from email addresses you've approved. The regular email address registered with your Amazon account is already added to the approved list.

To edit your **Approved Personal Document Email** list:

1. Visit **Manage Your Content and Devices** at www.amazon.com/mycd and click **Personal Document Settings**.

2. Under **Approved Personal Document Email** list, select **Add** a new approved email address.

3. Enter the new email address and click **Add Address**.

## Converting Documents

One of the best features of the Personal Documents Service is that it can automatically convert most common document formats to the Kindle format, called AZW. You don't have to know the technical details, it just works. Then once the document is on your Kindle, you can use many of the functions available with Kindle documents—you can make annotations, change the font, adjust the text size, and so forth. To convert your documents, enter the word Convert in the subject line of the email.

**TIP:** Don't use Personal Documents Service for commercial purposes, such as sending out a commercial newsletter. It's against Amazon's terms of service, and that's why it's called the Personal Documents Service.

## Transfer Personal Documents via USB Cable

Let's say you want to transfer a document from your computer to your Kindle via USB cable, and you need to convert the document to Kindle's .azw format. Before you can accomplish this, you'll need to change your Send-to-Kindle email address to the name [your-name]@free.kindle.com and then enter "convert" in the subject line of your email.

To download the converted document to your computer, follow the instructions Amazon puts in the email.

Choose your desktop, then click **Save**.

Connect your Kindle to your computer with the USB cable. (On a Windows computer, navigate to the Kindle by browsing My Computer. (On Macs, the Kindle will appear on your desktop.)

Click on the Kindle to browse the Kindle's drive.

Drag your document from your desktop and drop it into the **Documents** folder of the Kindle drive.

Eject your Kindle device and unplug the USB cable.

## Supported File Types for Kindle Personal Documents Service

The following file types can be automatically converted to the Kindle format .azw by sending them in an email with "convert" in the subject line:

Microsoft Word (.doc, .docx)

HTML (.html, .htm)

RTF (.rtf)

Text (.txt)

JPEG (.jpeg, .jpg)

Kindle Format (.mobi, .azw)

GIF (.gif)

PNG (.png)

BMP (.bmp)

PDF (.pdf)

## *'Send to Kindle' Application*

Another way to send documents to your Kindle is by using the **Send to Kindle** application, a free program you can install on your computer. With it, you can send content such as word-processing documents, news articles, blog posts and other content to your Kindle.

The Send-to-Kindle application is quite efficient and easy to use, and it automatically converts documents to the Kindle format.

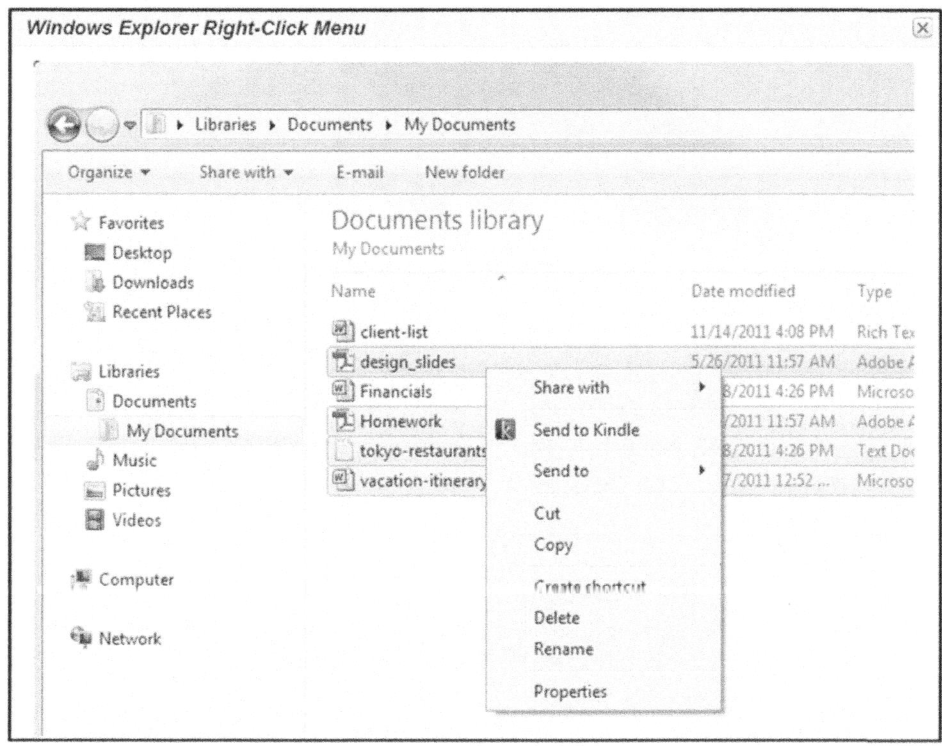


**Above: Using the right-click function of the Send-to-Kindle for PC application.**

Download the program by visiting www.amazon.com/gp/sendtokindle and following the instructions. After entering your Amazon email address and password, click **Register**. If you own more than one Kindle device, you can select which device(s) will receive the documents.

Send-to-Kindle is also available as a browser extension for the Chrome and Firefox Web browsers.

## Download From the Cloud

All of your Kindle content is saved to the Cloud and available for download to your Voyage. Let's imagine that you want to download a previously purchased Kindle book to your Voyage.

From the **Home** screen, tap **Books** to open its content library.

Tap **Cloud** (instead of **Device**) to display the books you own that haven't been downloaded to your Kindle.

Tap the **book** image to download it to your device. Items that have been downloaded to your Voyage have a check mark in the lower right corner of the cover image. Items stored in the Cloud do not have a check mark.

# 5 ▶ ADVANCED TIPS AND TRICKS

Once you've accumulated a few dozen books and other documents, it becomes hard to find what you're looking for. Perhaps you need a special place where you can pigeon-hole the 27 Thanksgiving cookbooks scattered throughout your Voyage. Fortunately, there's a solution: organizing those items into custom categories stored in the Cloud. You can add as many items as you wish to these **Cloud Collections**, including books, personal documents, and active content. (Newspapers, magazines and blogs can't be added to collections.)

## *Organize your content with Cloud Collections*

1.  To create a new collection:

    *   From **Home**, tap the **Menu** ☰ icon, then tap **Create New Collection**.

    *   Enter a name for the collection, then tap **OK**. A list appears of items eligible to be added to the collection.

    *   Tap the checkbox next to a title to add it to the collection.

    *   Tap **Done** when finished. The new collection will show up on the **Home** screen.

2.  To edit or delete a collection:

    *   From **Home**, press and hold the collection title.

    *   Tap to **Add/Remove Items**, **Rename This Collection**, or **Delete This Collection**.

Deleting a collection doesn't erase a book or other documents from your Kindle library. However, if you delete a collection, that collection is also deleted from the Cloud and your other Kindle devices and apps.

## *Viewing and Managing Your Cloud Collections*

Once you've established a few Cloud Collections, you'll probably want to customize the way you view and access them on your Voyage. You can also **star** your favorites to make them even more accessible.

1.  To filter your items on the Home screen:

    *   From **Home**, tap **My Items**. You'll see options to view **All Items** or only **Books**, **Periodicals**, **Docs**, **Collections**, or **Active Content**.

    *   Tap **Collections** to view all your collections.

2.  To star a collection:

- Press and hold a collection cover, then tap **Show in All Views**. A star appears in the bottom-right corner of the collection cover. The collection will appear on your Home screen when you view **All Items** or **Collections**. The collection also appears when you view **Books, Docs,** or **Active Content** if it contains books, personal documents, or active content, respectively.

3. To unstar a collection:

- Press and hold a starred collection cover, then tap **Show Only in Collections View**. A star will no longer appear on the collection cover, and the collection will only appear on your Home screen when you view **Collections**.

## *Fixing a Slow or Frozen Screen*

If your screen is slow to respond or freezes, try rebooting your device. Press and hold the power button for about five seconds. When the prompt appears on your screen, tap **Restart**. (Don't worry, restarting will not remove content or deregister your device.)

If the trouble persists, check your battery level and the cleanliness of your screen. Keep in mind, your device may respond slowly while downloading large items. Also, check to see if your device is using the most recent software updates. For more information, see the address below:

www.amazon.com/gp/help/customer/display.html?nodeId=200529680

The last resort in fixing a frozen Voyage is resetting the device to the factory default settings.

1. From the **Home** screen, tap the **Menu** ≡ icon.

2. Tap **Settings**.

3. Tap **Menu** again, then tap **Reset Device**.

After resetting, you'll need to register your device again and download content from your Kindle library.

## *Restrict access to your Kindle by setting a passcode*

For privacy's sake, or to disable your Kindle in the event it's lost or stolen, set a passcode.

1. From the **Home** screen, tap the Menu icon, ≡ .

2. Tap **Settings**, then tap **Device Options**.

3. Tap **Device Passcode**. Using the on-screen keyboard, enter and confirm a password.

4. Tap **OK**.

## *If you forget your device passcode*

If you can't recall your passcode, you'll need to reset your Voyage. This will remove your passcode, Amazon account information, and content you've downloaded.

1. Tap the passcode field.

2. Using the onscreen keyboard, type 111222777, then tap OK. Your Voyage will restart. Connect to a wireless network, re-register your device, and download the desired content from the Cloud.

## *Deregister Your Voyage*

If your Voyage is registered to the wrong Amazon account—or if you're no longer going to use it to buy content, you can deregister the device from your Amazon account. You can deregister while using your device, or while at Amazon's website.

After deregistering the device, you will no longer have access to your Kindle library or items previously downloaded through Kindle applications running on your smartphone or other devices.

After the deregistration process, you can Register the device to a different Amazon account.

From your device:

1. From the **Home** screen, tap the **Menu** ☰ icon, then tap **Settings**.

2. Tap **Registration**.

3. In the **Deregister Your Kindle** box, tap **Deregister**.

From your computer:

1. Visit Manage Your Content and Devices at www.amazon.com/mycd and then click **Your Devices**.

2. Click the image of your Voyage, then click **Deregister**.

## *Set up Parental Controls*

If you have young children in the home, the Parental Controls settings will provide you with peace of mind while your child uses the Kindle. You can restrict access to the Kindle store, shopping, and the web browser. When Parental Controls are enabled, the ability to deregister and reset your Voyage is disabled.

1. From **Home**, tap the Menu ☰ icon, then tap **Settings**.

2. Tap **Device Options**, then tap **Parental Controls**.

3. Tap **Off** to require a password to the web browser, Kindle store, or cloud.

4. Provide a Parental Controls password, then tap **OK**.

5.  Tap OK to save your Parental Controls settings.

When Parental Controls are set, a **lock** 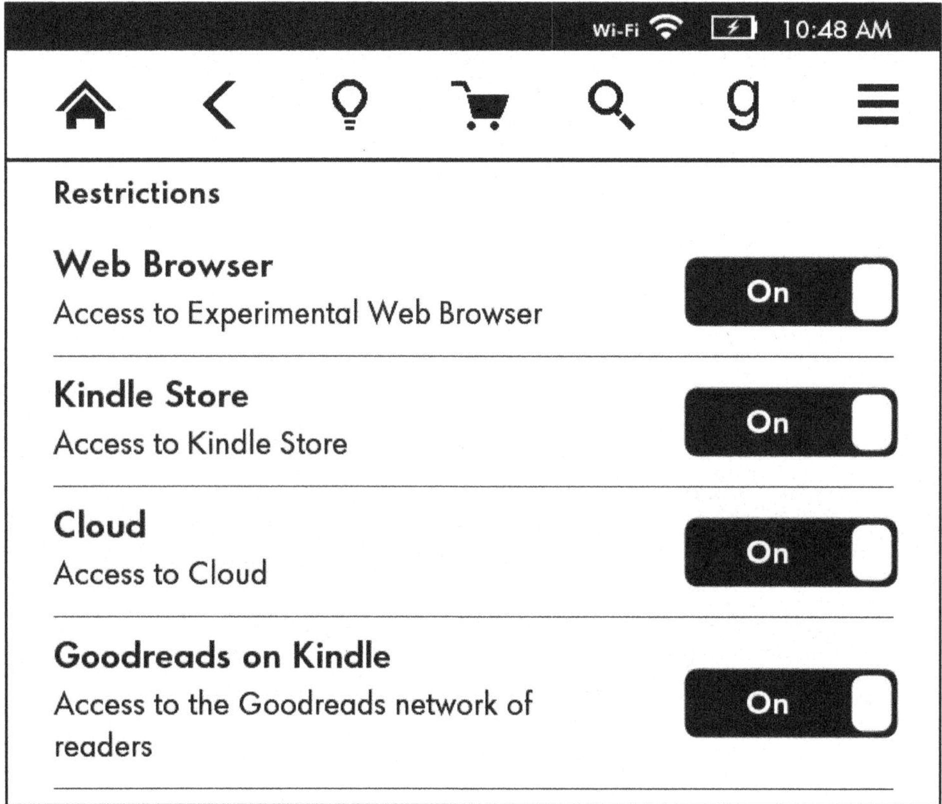 icon appears at the top of the screen.



**Above: With Parental Controls, you can prevent accidental access to the store and web browser.**

When access to the Kindle Store is locked on your Voyage, you can continue purchasing and delivering content from your computer.

## Transferring Content From a Computer to Your Voyage

In addition to WiFi, you can also use a USB cord to transfer files from your computer to your Voyage. First, we'll download a document from your Kindle library to your computer, then to your Kindle device:

1.  Visit **Manage Your Content and Devices** at http://www.amazon.com/mycd .

2.  Highlight the **Your Content** folder.

3.  Locate the content you wish to transfer, and click on box under the **Select** heading. A checkmark is created in the Select field.

4.  Slick on the box under the **Actions** heading.

5. From the drop-down menu that appears, click **Download & transfer via USB**.

6. Click **Download**.

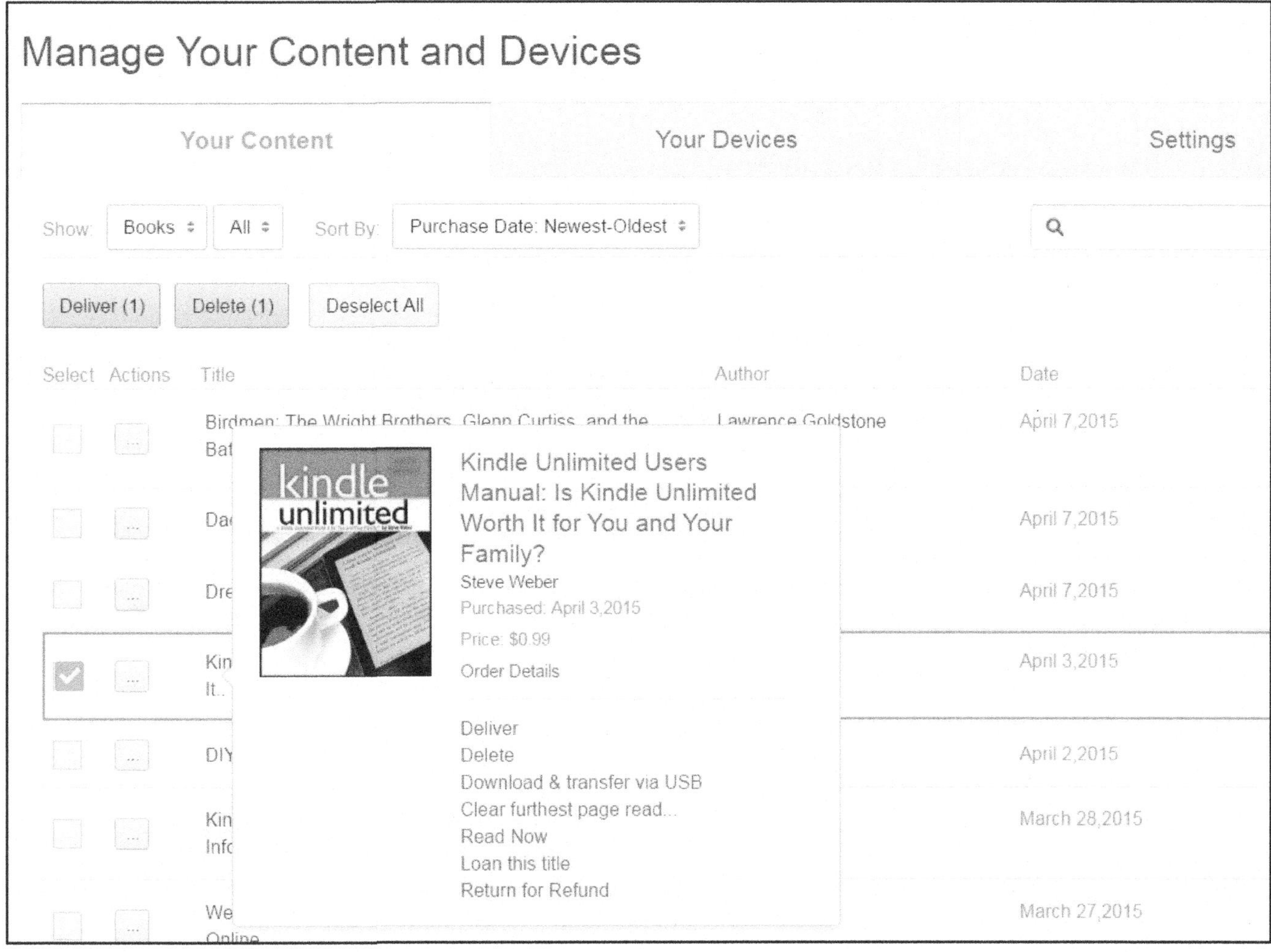

**Above: Downloading a file from the "Manage Your Content and Devices" page.**

Now we'll transfer the document from your computer to your Kindle via USB:

1. Connect your Kindle to your computer using the USB cord. (On Windows computers, your Kindle will appear in the same location as external USB drives, usually the **My Computer** menu. On Macs, your Kindle will appear on the desktop.)

2. Locate the downloaded file on your computer, then drag and drop the file into the **Documents** folder in the Kindle folder.

3. Eject your Kindle from your computer by right-clicking your Kindle and selecting **Eject**.

4. On your Kindle, tap **Home** 🏠 and **On Device** to view your content.

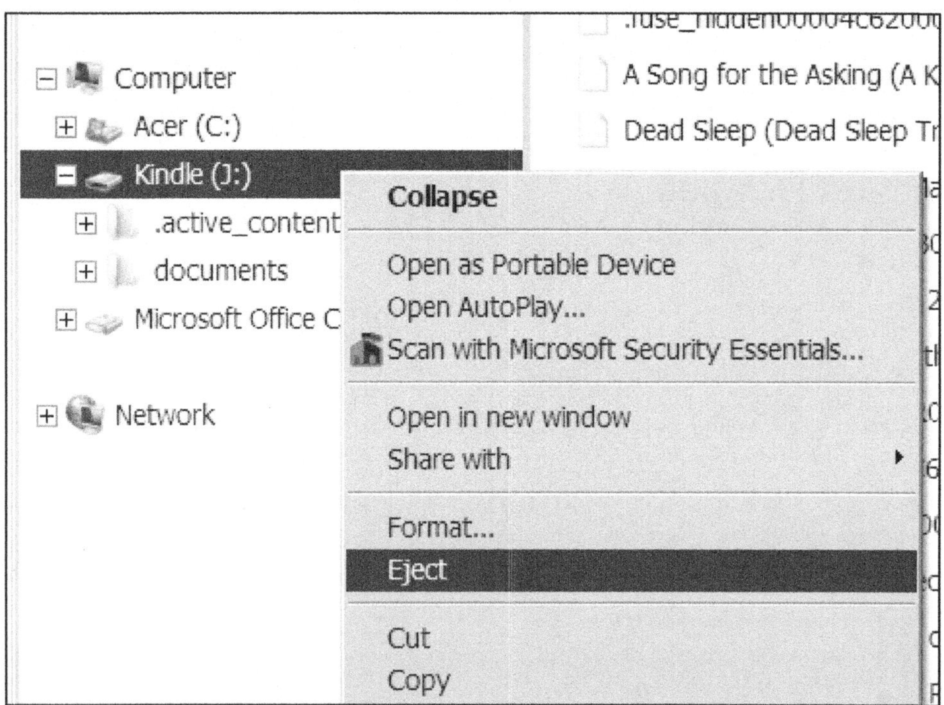

**Above: Ejecting the Voyage from a PC. Right-click the mouse pointer on the image of your Kindle device, then click "Eject."**

## *Change Your Device Language*

You can set your default language to English (U.S.), English (U.K.), German, French (France), French (Canada), Italian, Spanish (Spain), Spanish (Mexico), Portuguese (Brazil), Japanese, and Chinese (Simplified).

1.  From **Home**, tap the **Menu** ≡ icon, then tap **Settings**.

2.  Tap **Device Options**, then tap **Language and Dictionaries**, then tap one of these options:

    * **Language:** Pick a different language for your device.

    * **Keyboard:** Pick a region-specific layout for the keyboard.

    * **Dictionaries:** Set the default dictionary for each language.

When you pick a new language, the device menus, keyboard, and default dictionary are changed accordingly. If you purchase a book in a different language, the dictionary and keyboard for that language is downloaded to your Voyage automatically. The default dictionary and keyboard changes based on the language of the book you're reading.

## Enjoy Enhanced Reading Features

Simply reading a book is just scratching the surface when it comes to the Voyage. You can learn more about the book, easily look up words in the dictionary, and translate text.

### *Exploring Books with X-Ray*

X-Ray lets you explore the structure of a book. You can also dig for more background information from Wikipedia and Shelfari, Amazon's community for book lovers. X-Ray isn't available for all books—if it's not available, the X-Ray option is grayed out.

1.  While reading, tap the top of the screen to display the reading toolbar, then tap **X-Ray**.

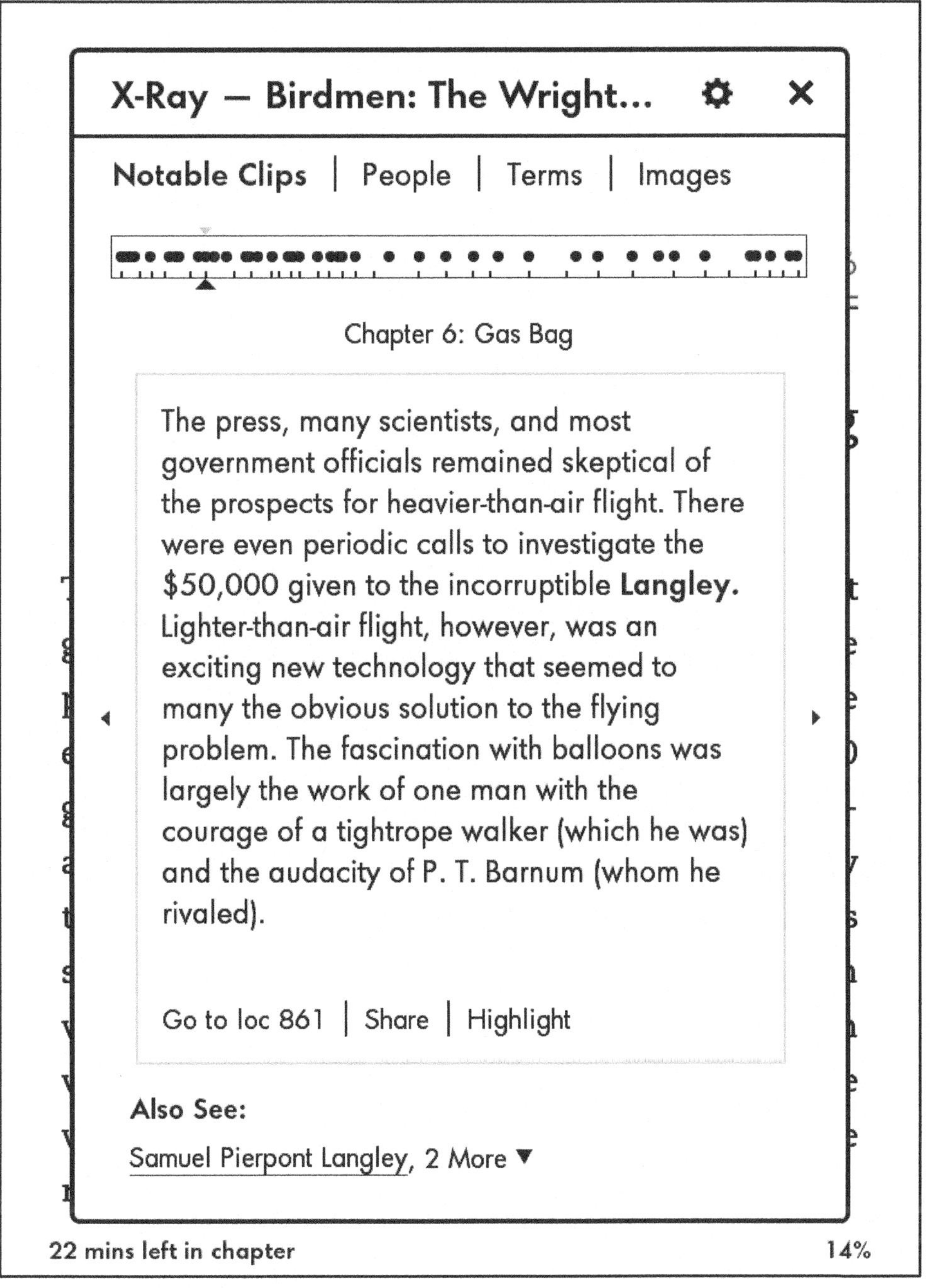

2.  View and filter the list of topics:

   - To filter by section of the book, tap **Notable Clips**, **People, Terms** or **Images.**

3.  To learn more about a topic or character, tap the item in the list. Then you can read a description, see links to Wikipedia or Shelfari, or excerpts in the book mentioning the term.

4.  When you're finished, tap the Back ❮ button or the **X** to resume reading.

**TIP:** Here's a shortcut to these enhanced features: While reading, press and hold a word or character name to launch the **Smart Lookup** window, where you can view Dictionary, X-Ray or Wikipedia information. Smart Lookup classifies the type of term you're looking up, and adjust the tabs accordingly.


## Use the Dictionary

One of the most powerful features of the Kindle is the ease of accessing dictionary definitions. Instead of interrupting your reading to grab a dictionary from your bookshelf, you can access instant information from the Voyage's built-in dictionary.

1.  While reading, press and hold a word, then release to launch the **Smart Lookup** window.

2.  Scroll within the **Dictionary** tab to view the full definition.

3.  Tap outside the window to resume reading.


## Expand Your Vocabulary

When you look up words in your Voyage's dictionary, they're automatically added to the **Vocabulary Builder** on the device. This feature generates flashcards, which you can use to test your retention of word definitions and usages.

1.  From **Home**, tap the **Menu** ☰ icon, then tap **Vocabulary Builder**. You'll see a list of all words you've looked up with the dictionary. There are separate tabs for **Books** (words you looked up within a specific book), **Learning** (words available as flashcards) and **Mastered** (words you marked as "mastered" and no longer included in flashcards).

2.  Tap **Flashcards** at the bottom of the screen to begin testing yourself of the list of words.

3.  To turn off **Vocabulary Builder**, tap the **Menu** ☰ icon, tap **Settings**, tap **Reading Options**, then tap **Vocabulary Builder**. While it's turned off, new words won't be added.

## *Translate Text with Instant Translations*

While reading, you can select text, then use **Instant Translations** to see the text in a different language.

1. While reading, press and drag to highlight the text you want to translate.

2. In the pop-up menu, tap **More**, tap **Translation**, and then select the language you want the text translated to.

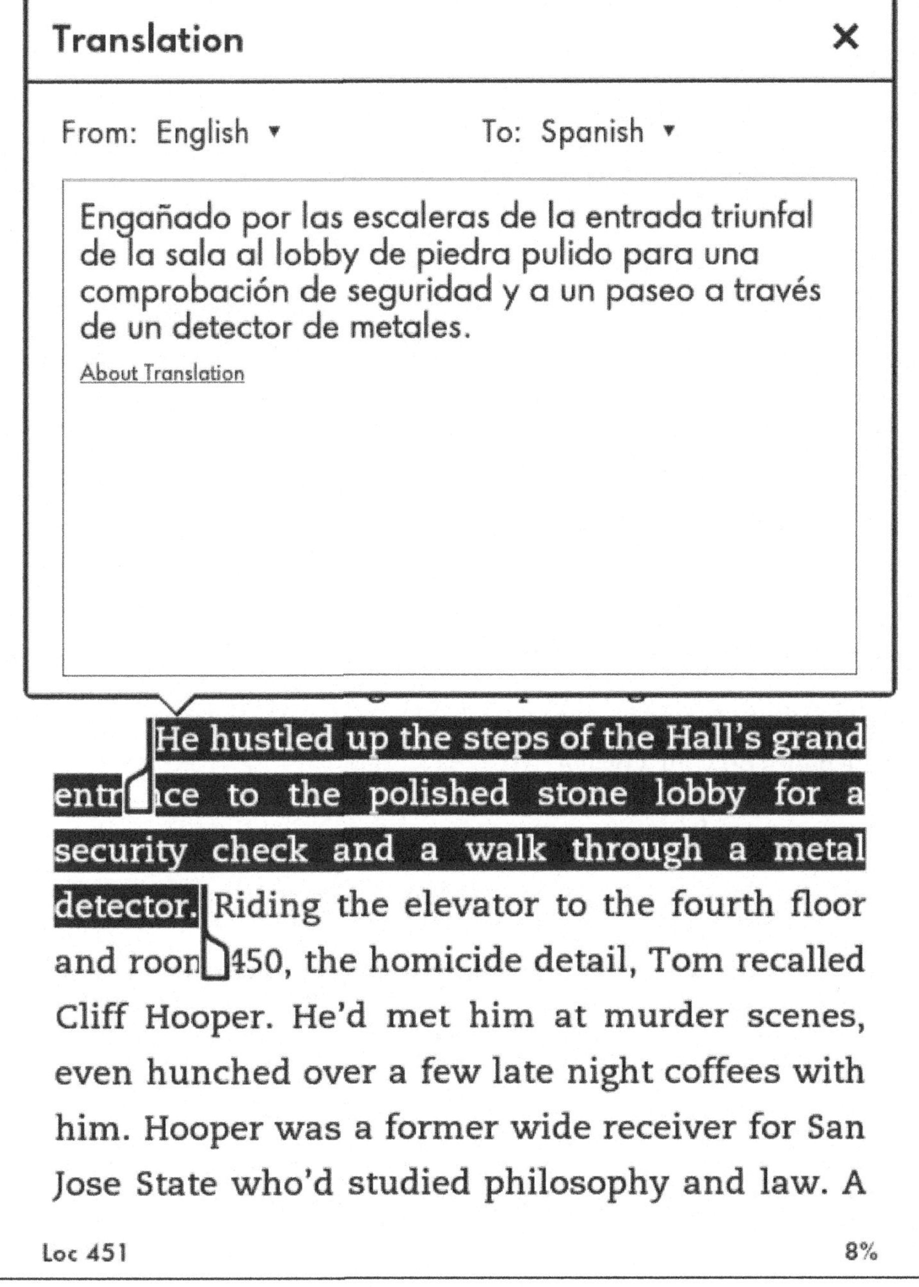

### *Set Up Kindle FreeTime*

If you have a young child in the home, consider setting up Kindle FreeTime by setting a Parental Controls password and creating a profile for your child. Kindle FreeTime automatically blocks access to the Kindle store, the web browser, and Wikipedia. Children can only read books you've added to their library.

1. From Home, tap the **Menu** ☰ icon, then tap **Kindle Freetime**.

2. Tap **Get Started**.

3. Enter a password. This password is the same as your Parental Controls password, if you've already created one.

4. Enter your child's name, date of birth, and gender, then tap **Next**. A list of the titles in **Your Kindle Library** appears. (The personal information is used only to tailor the user experience.)

5. Tap the checkbox next to a title to add it to your child's **FreeTime** library, then tap **OK**. (Public library books, personal documents, and books from the Kindle Owner's Lending Library can't be added to a FreeTime profile.)

6. Set your child's **Access to Achievements** and **Daily Reading Goal**. By default, the daily goal is set to 30 minutes.

7. Tap **Finish** to save all settings and create the profile.


### *Find and Share Books on Goodreads*

Goodreads is an online book community owned by Amazon where you can follow friends to see what they're reading, and share and rate books on your Voyage.

1. From **Home**, tap the **Goodreads** g icon.

2. Connect your Amazon account to Goodreads using one of these two options:

   - If you already have a Goodreads account, tap **Connect Existing Account**.

   - If you don't already have a Goodreads account, tap **Create New Account**.

3. Tap +**Follow** beside readers you want to follow, then tap **Next**.

4. Add your Amazon books to shelves or rate your books to add them to Goodreads, then tap **Next**. Rate books by tapping the desired numbers of stars next to the book.

## *Link your Voyage to Facebook or Twitter*

You can share your reading status, notes, book highlights, and book ratings on Facebook or Twitter. You can link or unlink your device to these social networks at any time.

1.  From **Home**, tap the **Menu** ☰ icon, then tap **Settings**.

2.  Tap **Reading Options**, then tap **Social Networks**.

3.  Tap **Link Account** or **Unlink Account** and follow the on-screen instructions.

## *Manage Your Subscription Settings*

You can make changes to your subscriptions to magazines, newspapers and blogs.

1.  Visit **Manage Your Content and Devices** at www.amazon.com/mycd

2.  Under **Your Kindle Account**, click **Subscription Settings**.

3.  On the **Subscription Settings** page, click the **Actions** button next to the title, then you can:

- Deliver past issues of subscription content to an eligible Kindle device or app.

- Cancel a subscription

- Download a title or issue of a subscription to your computer, then transfer it to your Kindle via USB cable.

- Choose privacy preferences, such as whether to share your email address with subscription publishers.

## *Edit Device Names*

The name of your device is set automatically by Amazon, but you can change the name of the device to make it more meaningful. For example, when my most recent Kindle Voyage arrived in its box, Amazon named it "Steve's 6th Kindle." I changed the name to "Steve's New Voyage" so that I can distinguish it from my several other Kindle devices purchased earlier.

The device name appears at the upper left corner of your device screen and on the **Manage Your Content and Devices** page. Here's how to edit the name of your device:

1.  Visit **Manage Your Content and Devices** at www.amazon.com/mycd

2.  Click **Manage Your Devices**.

3.  Click **Edit** beside the name of the device or app.

4.  Enter the desired name and click **Update**.

## *Delete Items From Your Kindle Library*

If you want to free up space on your Kindle device, you can tap its icon once, then tap **Remove From Device**. If you wish, you'll be able to send the item to your Kindle at a future point. By contrast, **if you delete an item from your Kindle library, the action is permanent**—you won't be able to download the item again unless you buy it again.

1. Visit **Manage Your Content and Devices** at www.amazon.com/mycd

2. Locate the item you want to delete.

3. From the **Actions** drop-down menu, select **Delete from library**. Confirm by clicking **Yes**.

Made in the USA
Monee, IL
09 January 2022

88536186R00037